MAPS OF TEXAS
AND THE
SOUTHWEST

J. De Cordova's Map of the State of Texas, 1849.

MAPS OF TEXAS AND THE SOUTHWEST, 1513-1900

James C. Martin
Robert Sidney Martin

PUBLISHED FOR THE AMON CARTER MUSEUM
by the
UNIVERSITY OF NEW MEXICO PRESS
Albuquerque

Library of Congress Cataloging in Publication Data

Martin, James C.
  Maps of Texas and the Southwest, 1513–1900.

  "Prepared in conjunction with an exhibition produced by the Amon Carter Museum, Fort Worth . . ."—Verso t.p.
  Includes index.
  Bibliography: p.
  1. Texas—Maps. 2. Cartography—Texas—History. 3. Texas—Historical geography—Maps. 4. Texas—History. 5. Southwest, Old—Maps. 6. Maps—Facsimiles. I. Martin, Robert Sidney. II. Amon Carter Museum of Western Art. III. Title.
G1370.M3   1984   912'.764   84-675055

The Amon Carter Museum was established in 1961 under the will of the late Amon G. Carter for the study and documentation of westering North America. The program of the museum, expressed in permanent collections, exhibitions, publications, and special events, reflects many aspects of American culture, both historic and contemporary.

This book was prepared in conjunction with the exhibit "Crossroads of Empire: Printed Maps of Texas and the Southwest, 1513–1900" produced by the Amon Carter Museum, Fort Worth, and co-sponsored by the Cartographic History Library, The University of Texas at Arlington; and the San Jacinto Museum of History, Houston; and supported by a grant from Justin Industries, Fort Worth.

CONTENTS

ILLUSTRATIONS

PREFACE

The task of summarizing the growth of the geographical knowledge about the land we know as Texas for a period of four centuries—the scope of this volume—must suffer from many obvious, and some less apparent, obstacles. Such a challenge demands familiarity with not only the general history of the period, but also a broad understanding of historical cartography as well. The wide range of related disciplines, including geography, astronomy, navigation, printing, ethnology, and languages, present demands and discouragement to such a study. Fortunately one can enjoy historical cartography on many levels and with differing degrees of sophistication, and maps themselves hold a wide variety of pleasures—from their simplistic beauty to their sometimes hidden treasures of information available only to the trained eye.

The present study grew out of research for the first exhibition detailing the historical cartography of Texas, which traveled to libraries and museums throughout the region. That exhibit, "Crossroads of Empire," was the most extensive ever, a result of the foresight of Justin Industries and the staff of the Amon Carter Museum. Because of the admitted complexity of the project, our first goal in selecting the maps and in writing this text has been to stimulate further inquiry and to add to the appreciation of the value of historic maps as tools in learning about any place, in any time.

In working with many institutions and people we have enjoyed splendid cooperation and encouragement. In addition to the generous lenders to the exhibition, listed separately, we ac-knowledge gratefully the leadership and direction of Dr. Ron Tyler and the special support of Jan Muhlert, Director of the Amon Carter Museum; Preston Figley of Fort Worth, who gave early and unlimited assistance; Robert W. Karrow of the Newberry Library; Richard W. Stephenson of the Geography and Map Division, Library of Congress; Dr. Don Carlton and Mrs. Frances Rodgers of the Barker Texas History Center, The University of Texas at Austin; Joe B. Frantz, Professor of History, University of Texas at Austin; Dr. Tuffly Ellis, Director of the Texas State Historical Association; John Hudson, Charles Harrell, and the staff of the Division of Special Collections at The University of Texas at Arlington Library; John Hyatt and Mrs. Jane Kenamore of the Rosenberg Library; Mr. and Mrs. Jenkins Garrett of Fort Worth, leaders in the founding of the Cartographic History Library at The University of Texas at Arlington; Paul G. Bell, President of the San Jacinto Museum of History Association, and Mrs. Aileen Szymborski, Mrs. Ruth Roberts, and Winston Atkins of the Museum staff; and finally we wish to remember the late James Perry Bryan, Sr., whose enthusiasm for the study of the cartographic history of Texas directly initiated the studies produced here, and whose map library housed in the Barker Texas History Center, The University of Texas at Austin, should stimulate and support many future studies.

ROBERT S. MARTIN
J. C. MARTIN

LENDERS TO THE EXHIBITION

Amon Carter Museum, Ft. Worth, Texas
Barker Texas History Center, The University of Texas at Austin
Mr. Paul G. Bell, Houston, Texas
Cartographic History Library, The University of Texas at Arlington
Christensen/Byram Collection, Austin, Texas
Mr. and Mrs. Jenkins Garrett, Ft. Worth, Texas
Jenkins Garrett Library, The University of Texas at Arlington
Library of Congress, Washington, D.C.
The Newberry Library, Chicago, Illinois
Mr. Herman Pressler, Houston, Texas
Mr. Paul C. Ragsdale, New Braunfels, Texas
The Rosenberg Library, Galveston, Texas
San Jacinto Museum of History Association, Houston, Texas
Mr. F. Carrington Weems, Houston, Texas

MAPS OF TEXAS
AND THE
SOUTHWEST

INTRODUCTION

The Gulf of Mexico, its sister seas and waterways, captured the hopes and expectations of European nations to find new avenues to wealth and power when Columbus first reported its discovery. Initial promises for an easier, cheaper passageway to the riches of Asia quickly vanished with the realization that a new world blocked the way. The two continents surrounding this body of water at once overwhelmed imagination and transformed the search for new trade routes into an almost frantic rush to territorial claims. Nations were eager to exploit the newly revealed and seemingly unlimited treasures of natural resources. The royal courts, the Church, the soldier-adventurer, the scientist—all studied these new lands as special opportunities for the advancement of their particular cause. The resulting intense demand for knowledge of the New World reached into every detail of human activity, altering the course of some, and destroying others.

Few events in human history could equal the impact of these discoveries. From the outset, Europeans realized that the geographical knowledge held by one nation would result in a decisive disadvantage for another. The Papal Bull of 1493 dividing the New World into halves for Portugal and Spain failed to reduce the spirit of rivalry among all nations having the naval facilities to compete. The discoveries of Spain and Portugal in the southern half of this new hemisphere led to the long-sought avenue to the East with the circumnavigation of the globe by Ferdinand Magellan between 1519 and 1522. In addition, the conquest of Mexico by Hernando Cortés in 1521 ensured the prominence of Spain in the Gulf region. England and France hoped to check the claims of the Iberian powers with the exploration of the Hudson Bay area, the lands drained by the Mississippi River, and the northern continent's eastern seaboard, and with their advance toward the Florida peninsula.

The borderlands in between—the lands yet unexplored by the conquerors and therefore left largely untouched and undefined in their claims—became known on maps alternately as Nueva España, La Florida, La Louisiane, Carolana (a British claim adjacent to Carolina), Nuevo México, and Nuevas Filipinas. The heart of these lands became known as Texas.

Competition, exacerbated by each nation's ignorance of the natural geography of the territories it claimed, precipitated a rush to record its explorations—and equally important, those of its rivals—in an effort to achieve political and economic advantages. This territorial rivalry persisted for four centuries, during which time the lands involving the overlapping claims of Spain and France became a focal point in the international struggle that eventually produced a new nation, Texas, and later provided the United States with the opportunity to more than double its size and its relative importance in the international community.

The competition also significantly encouraged, in Europe and later in America, the production and refinement of maps of North America in general, and of its regions in particular. Although the need for accurate maps constantly supported the growth of the cartographical sciences, political motives were never far from the minds of many of the map makers. In fact, a number of the maps of lasting importance were produced to document the claims of a European sovereign.

To the student of history, however, cartographic productions have been far more important than mere documents of territorial claims. They have represented graphic illustrations of what man has known about his world at any particular time. Through historic maps, for example, the state of geographical knowledge has been immediately available to the casual observer and the seasoned specialist alike. Advances in technology and in the relevant sciences become visually apparent as well. Finally, the finished map, carefully researched, immaculately printed, and frequently hand-colored, has become a window into the cartographer's attitude about himself, his art, and the world he depicts. Long used, if not always designed, as vehicles of communication among peoples and nations, historic maps, when viewed together, can present accurate as well as aesthetically pleasing statements about our past.

THE SCIENCE OF MAP MAKING

Man has always made maps. At least from that point in human development when records of transactions began to appear and prehistory gave way to the historical period, maps have been among those permanent documents. The earliest maps were but crude sketches scratched on the rock or clay writing surfaces of the fourth millennium before Christ, describing the extent of individual plots of land. But the makers of maps quickly became more ambitious and the scope of their representations grew with their increasing awareness and knowledge of the world around them.

As an image of the earth's surface, a map presents several fundamental problems in its construction: those of depicting two or more points on the earth's surface, in proper relationship to each other, on a two dimensional surface and at a reduced scale. The fact that the surface of the earth is a sphere, while the surface of a map is usually a plane, further complicates the problem and introduces the need for various projections for properly depicting the image contrived by the map maker. The early creation of an accurate map, therefore, required a thorough understanding of astronomy and mathematics, the combination of which resulted in the development of the science of cartography.

Cartography as a science was not born full-fledged; it developed slowly from obscure origins, enjoying its first great flowering in the last century before Christ in Alexandria, the Roman capital of Egypt. It was there for the first time that scholars first worked out the relationship between geography and astronomy. The early Greek astronomer and polymath Strabo, from whose writings we learn most of what we know about science in ancient Alexandria, noted that anyone who wished to learn the basics of geography, including the general character of the earth, its size and shape, and the relationship of the inhabited versus the uninhabited parts, "must first look to the heavens." By observing the stars and the planets the ancients learned much about the earth, its place in the universe and the nature of its surface.

Pythagoras showed as early as 500 B.C. that the earth is a sphere. Aristarchus of Samos first put forth the idea that the earth orbited about the sun in 300 B.C. In the third century B.C., Eratosthenes, by noting the difference of the angular height of the sun in two separate places at the same time, calculated the circumference of the earth to within five hundred miles of its actual value, and thus computed the length of a degree of longitude. The observation of the heavens was thus early established as the key to accurately describing the surface of the earth.

The greatest of the ancient geographers was Claudius Ptolemy, who flourished in Alexandria about A.D. 150. Building on the knowledge of his predecessors, Ptolemy constructed a system of geography that was accepted virtually unrevised for nearly fifteen hundred years. The publication of his *Geography*, a landmark in map making, set forth for the first time the tenets of cartography. Ptolemy not only defined cartography and geography, described the duties and routines of the map maker, designed instruments for celestial observations, and specified the construction of two different map projections, but he also prescribed the directions for making the first uniform set of maps of the known world.

Ptolemy made his greatest contribution in propounding a scientific approach to map making entirely modern in spirit. Having perfected the existing mathematics and applied its principles to the problems of map construction, he demonstrated more clearly than any of his predecessors the numerous feasible methods of applying the findings of astronomy to the study of the earth. He also systematized the principles and techniques for mapping the earth's surface and originated many of the conventional signs and symbols still in use in maps today. For example, Ptolemy initiated the practice of orienting maps with the north at the top, a practice which has taken such a strong hold that most individuals find it difficult to make sense of a map oriented otherwise. What mistakes Ptolemy made were due to an absence

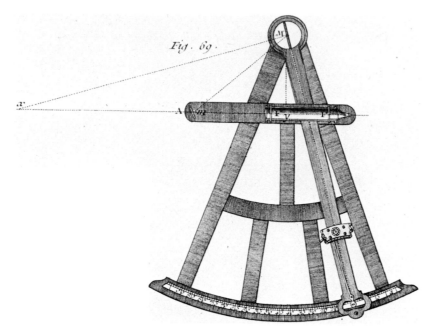

Fig. 69.

Eighteenth century sextant; from Denis Diderot, *Encyclopédie, ou dictionnaire raisonné des sciences, des arts, et des métiers* (Paris, 1751–56).

by mystical introspection, theological exegesis, and metaphorical models of reality. As Lloyd Brown states in *The Story of Maps*, "The lamp of scientific knowledge, a tremulous flame at best was obscured for a time by the blinding light of religious ecstasy."

Medieval cartography, therefore, followed primarily Christian designs, and became an amalgam of folklore, theological explanations of the universe, and an assortment of geographical statistics transcribed from ancient itineraries. The Medieval world view was conditioned by Pliny and Solinus, and the maps of the period were stylized depictions with allegorical intent, such as the so-called T-O maps of Isidore of Seville. These maps described the known world with an O-shaped ocean, divided into three continents by three major waterways, the Don and Nile rivers and the Mediterranean Sea, drawn in the shape of a T.

The other-worldly orientation of the Middle Ages began to come apart under the impetus of new geographical knowledge that accumulated during the Crusades. Armies and pilgrims returning to Europe brought back new information not only about the Holy Land and other places they had actually visited, but also what they had learned by contact with merchants and traders from Arabia, India, Africa, and even China. Travelers such as the Polo brothers added even further to geographical information. By the fourteenth century, expanding trade between Europe and the Orient added a new impetus to navigation and exploration as the Mediterranean nations vied with each other for more efficient routes to the East. The Portuguese under Prince Henry began to push the frontiers of the known world south and west from the pillars of Hercules in search of new markets, and their discoveries were evident in the detailed sailing charts of the period, known as portolanos.

As Mediterranean ships began to venture farther from the known shores and to ply the waters of the Atlantic, the need to determine their precise position mothered corresponding advances in navigation. The compass was adopted from the Chinese,

of hard facts available in the ancient world. His influence was so pervasive that the progress of cartography was, in fact, retarded temporarily when new information became available because it required revision of the Ptolemaic world view.

During the Middle Ages, the science of cartography, like all others in Western civilization, was converted to and encompassed by Christianity. The scientific knowledge of the ancients was subordinated to a preoccupation with spiritual salvation, and man's critical examination of the world around him was replaced and crude instruments for taking celestial observations were developed from the land-based experiments of the ancients. In the hands of a competent seaman, the astrolabe could enable him to determine his latitude with remarkable accuracy; this instrument improved progressively over the centuries, resulting in the cross-staff, the backstaff, the quadrant, the octant, and finally the sextant. The problem of determining a ship's position east and west, however, was more intractable, and for centuries this position was deduced from dead-reckoning. In this method the course and speed of the ship were combined to produce a rough estimate of the ship's position. Since speed was determined by the crude method of "throwing the log," and time was measured by the sands of the hourglass, the results of dead-reckoning were unreliable. This led inevitably to gross inaccuracies in the east-west coordinates on maps and charts. The search for a solution to the conundrum of calculating longitude led to the posting of prizes by the maritime powers, and experiments with various celestial observations including the relative positions of the moons of Jupiter were tried. These proved fruitless, and it was only with the development of an accurate chronometer or clock in the late eighteenth century that mariners were able to determine their longitude with any precision.

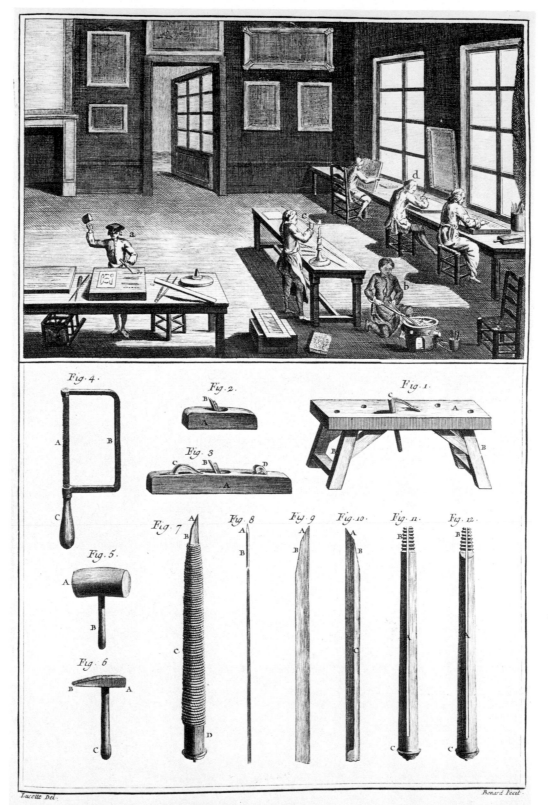

Woodcutting operations and tools;
from Diderot, *Encyclopédie*

MAP PRINTING

One of the remarkable coincidences of history during the great flowering of human creativity and endeavor known as the Renaissance was that the resurgence of interest in the world, which caused its exploration, also occurred along with the development of the art of printing. Thus maps, which were produced both as an aid and a consequence of discovery, could be more widely disseminated through multiple copies.

The printing of maps, however, presents several difficult problems. As a graphic image the map offers great possibilities for the compression of information; like a picture, one map can be worth a thousand words. But this graphic quality means that a map is quite different from printed text in several important respects. The letters of the alphabet have been thoroughly understood by the literate for many hundreds of years and, consequently, unless the type font used is eccentric, exceptionally ugly, or otherwise difficult to read, the reader absorbs the meaning of a printed text without much reaction to the graphic qualities of its format. A map, on the other hand, employs a complicated array of symbols and techniques for conveying its message, including, for example, lines, shading, tones, patterns, and even words. A map, then, is more complex than a page of text, and the reader reacts in important but subtle ways to its graphic characteristics. For this reason, the method used to print a map is extremely important in evaluating its origin and the information it conveys. Some methods are quite accommodating, allowing the cartographer to work closely with the printer in transferring the drawn image to its printed form, and in accepting the nuances of that image in all its variations. Other methods, though, are essentially resistant to the intention of the cartographer, interposing intermediaries between him and the printer, or adding to the difficulty in translating elements of the design through the printing process. The final result is that what might be called the "look" of a map is inseparable from the process by which it is printed; its success or failure is directly linked to its production technique.

The original method used for printing maps, developing from the medieval tradition of the block book, was the woodcut. In this relief process a flat surface, usually a block of wood, had the image drawn directly on it in reverse, and then the portions of the block not carrying the image were cut away, leaving a raised surface with the image. This block was then inked and the image was transferred to paper in a press. The process is similar to the familiar rubber stamp of today. Because of the difficulty of carving wood, particularly across the grain, the woodcut was a particularly resistant process and it is characterized by a distinct linearity and coarseness of image. Curves were particularly difficult to render, and tones were possible only in the crudest fashion. In addition, it was very hard to amend a woodblock except by removing a part of the image, and place names were also difficult to produce, usually being done through the use of metal types. On the other hand, the relief block had the advantage of being printed in the same press used to print the text which often accompanied maps, and in fact the map could be locked into the same chase with letterpress text and be printed on the same page. Nevertheless, its myriad disadvantages outweighed this single advantage, and the woodcut map was gradually phased out after 1550.

Replacing woodcuts in most of the map trade was the intaglio process, which offered a marked contrast. In this process, the image was incised into a smooth hard surface, frequently a copper plate. The plate was inked, then wiped clean, leaving ink only in the cracks and crevices of the incised image. The plate, with a dampened piece of paper, was then run through a roller press at high pressure and the ink was transferred to the paper. This process produced an image with vastly superior aesthetic qualities to the woodcut, with crisp, sharp lines and graceful curves. Tones were easily created through stippling or pecking the plate, and a wide variety of textures was possible. In addition, a copper plate was easily corrected. This attribute assumed major importance throughout the period of exploration and discovery when new information was continually made available and added to existing maps. The portion of the plate to be corrected was simply burnished smooth and re-engraved. Some maps were corrected over and over again, and the plates from which they were printed became an important asset in the printing trade. The intaglio process was, unfortunately, incompatible with the letter press, and consequently the preparation of text to accompany the maps involved a separate process, thus significantly increasing the cost of publishing a book with maps. The cost of copper and the labor-intensive process of engraving a set of plates at the hands of a skilled and experienced artisan meant that a substantial amount of capital was required to participate in the map trade. This necessity also distanced the cartographer from his map and increased the importance of the engraver and the publisher in the map-making process. Nevertheless, because of the many advantages of engraving, most maps were produced by this process between 1550 and 1850.

The dominance of the intaglio process persisted until the invention of lithography in the nineteenth century by Alois Senefelder. Based on the simple principle that oil and water do not mix, the planographic process known as lithography transfers an image to the paper from a smooth surface, instead of from a raised (relief) or incised (intaglio) surface. This is accomplished through chemical rather than physical action. The image is drawn on a smooth stone with grease or wax, the stone wet with water, then inked. The greasy ink adheres to the image lines but not to the wetted stone and transfers the image to a sheet of paper when run through a press. Lithography had the obvious advantages of simplicity and lower costs and therefore was adopted for

map printing on a large scale as early as 1820. Because any image that could be drawn could be lithographed, the medium returned the cartographer to a closer association with the finished map. While early lithographed maps imitated the visual characteristics of engraved maps, soon they came to have their own characteristic style. Zinc plates were substituted for stone, and power cylinder presses were introduced by the 1820s.

In spite of lithography's many advantages, it, like the intaglio process, was incompatible with the relief presses that produced the text. As printing presses became increasingly steam-driven and the printing business industrialized in the middle of the nineteenth century, it was possible for the first time, with power presses and cheap pulp paper, to produce vast quantities of books quickly and inexpensively. What was needed was a map-printing process that kept pace with the production of text, ideally in the same power presses. This need led to the development of the cerographic, or wax-engraving, process. Cerography was a complex process in which the image was first traced and engraved on a plate, then layers of wax were built up to make a relief image, which was then electroplated. This resulted in extremely hard and durable relief plate which could be printed in a power press. Lettering was easily accomplished through the use of type punches, and a distinct uniformity of lettering, combined with an unlimited selection of type faces, resulted in a complex but pleasing hierarchy in the place names on a map. Despite the complexity of the cerographic process the plates were relatively simple to correct and their compatibility with the power press made it an ideal process for the time. Wax-engraving was most successfully used in the industrialized American map trade, resulting in the development of what David Woodward has termed the "All-American Map." The process dominated the trade well into the twentieth century and until the development of modern photographic offset processes.

Eighteenth century intaglio roller-press; from Diderot, *Encyclopédie*

THE MAP TRADE

The development of movable type in the middle of the fifteenth century made it possible for the first time to print multiple, uniform copies of a work relatively cheaply. In response to eager demand, the business of printing spread rapidly, and printers soon began a search for material to print. They first turned to the material closest at hand, the classics, which had heretofore been available to the reading public only in expensive and scarce manuscript copies. One of the more frequently published classics during the incunabula period was the *Geography* of Ptolemy. The earliest printing of Ptolemy occurred within a decade of Gutenberg's Bible and was rapidly followed by six more editions in the next thirty years. These editions of Ptolemy included not only the text of the treatise but also various renditions of the maps it described, and with this revival of Ptolemy the modern map trade was born.

The discoveries and explorations of the early sixteenth century resulted in new knowledge to be incorporated into the maps of the period as well as vastly increasing the demand for maps portraying these new discoveries. The extension of geographical knowledge beyond that known to Ptolemy appeared first as appendixes to his work, beginning with the addition of a world map on which some hint of the new discoveries was depicted in the Rome printing of Ptolemy in 1507. Thirty-two additional editions of Ptolemy appeared before the end of the sixteenth century, each incorporating additional information and discoveries.

How new information gleaned from the voyages of discovery was disseminated is still not well understood. The maritime powers competed with each other for new territories and the vast riches of the New World. As a result, they often considered geographical knowledge a state secret. The Spanish were particularly secretive and as early as 1508 established the Casa de Contratación, which was responsible for receiving the mandated reports from each royally sponsored voyage and for coordinating the mapping of the new Spanish dominions. Much of the record of this endeavor is preserved in the Archives of the Indies at Seville. From that record it is clear that not only did the Spanish not share their information with others, but they frequently did not share it with themselves, resulting in many an exploratory enterprise being founded on misconception and many reports of explorers repeating the mistakes of their forebears. Naturally it also meant that the map publishers of Europe were often not privy to official or accurate information and were forced to rely on hearsay, unofficial reports, and the exaggerated stories of sailors.

Although printing had first blossomed in Italy and many of the early editions of Ptolemy bear Italian imprints, by the middle of the sixteenth century the center of map making had moved to the Netherlands. Here the great Dutch cartographer Gerhard Mercator worked, perfecting the projection that bears his name, and first applying the term *atlas* to a book of maps. Mercator was also the first to divide the New World into North and South, appending the name America to both continents. Earlier the name applied only to South America. It was also in the Netherlands that Mercator's friend, Abraham Ortelius, first abandoned the structures of the Ptolemaic system of geography when he published a book of maps in which uniform coverage was given to the entire world. Ortelius's 1570 *Theatrum Orbis Terrarum* (see Color Plate I; also Plate 4) has often been called the first modern atlas.

The discoveries of the New World created a flourishing shipping trade centered in Holland in which Dutch ships busied themselves plying back and forth from Lisbon and the northern parts of Europe and Britain, transshipping the wealth of the East. Charts and sailing directions were vital tools of this trade, and it was therefore natural that the Dutch should also have produced the first systematic collection of navigational charts bound into a book. This sea atlas was compiled and published over a number of years beginning in 1584 by Lucas Jansz Waghenaer. Entitled *The Mariner's Mirror*, it was so successful and definitive that for centuries sea atlases were known as "Waggoners."

The Dutch domination of the map trade continued into the seventeenth century. Mercator's plates were purchased by Jodocus Hondius in 1604, and the Mercator *Atlas* continued in print long after the master's death. Hondius was in turn succeeded by his sons, Jodocus and Henricus, and by his son-in-law, Jan Jansson (see Plate 8). Meanwhile, Willem Janszoon Blaeu set up shop in Amsterdam in 1596; by 1631 he was in full competition with the Hondius firm. Blaeu was succeeded in 1638 by his son, Joan Blaeu, whose *Atlas Major* in 1662 marked the apogee of the Dutch cartographic trade. The development of the Dutch sea atlases and pilot books was carried to its greatest achievements under the leadership of Johannes van Keulen and his son, Gerhard. These firms led the business of map and chart making, a business in which success depended on obtaining the most reliable and up-to-date information; therefore, in the days before international copyright, maps were plagiarized unabashedly. The very plates from which they were printed were jealously guarded and often became the subjects of sale, barter, and theft.

The Dutch hegemony in the cartographic enterprise gradually yielded during the seventeenth century to the French. Nicolas Sanson d'Abbeville, the first French Royal Geographer, produced maps incorporating the most accurate knowledge and scientific techniques of the time. After his death, his title was bestowed on Guillaume Delisle, whose scientific approach to map making resulted in the most accurate, influential, and often copied maps of the age. In the second half of the eighteenth century the leading French cartographer was Jean-Baptiste Bourguignon d'Anville whose maps were copied throughout the world.

By the end of the eighteenth century, as British world power increased, so too did British map making. Though England had early produced important cartographers—like Christopher Sax-

ton and John Speed—and expert navigational chart makers—like John Seller and John Thornton—English maps of the sixteenth and seventeenth centuries were for the most part either of English territories or copied from Dutch or French sources. The first great British cartographer of North America was John Mitchell, whose 1755 map has been called the most important map in American history. At the end of the eighteenth century, Aaron Arrowsmith introduced a new standard of excellence in map making and almost single-handedly made London the center for the cartographic trade. His maps of North America in particular served as models for twenty years. The British firms of John Arrowsmith, James Wyld, and John Cary retained the world prominence through the first half of the nineteenth century.

The American map trade began in earnest with Matthew Carey in Philadelphia in the 1790s. He was followed in that city by the firms of H. S. Tanner and Samuel Augustus Mitchell, while in New York J. H. Colton and Alvin J. Johnson were competing. All of these firms supplied maps and atlases to the eager market of settlers, travelers, land speculators, railroad men, and government officials as the nation made its inexorable drive to the West. In the second half of the nineteenth century, the Chicago firms of Rand, McNally, Hammond, and George F. Cram pioneered the development of the wax-engraving process and thus contributed to the modernization and industrialization of the map-printing trade.

The private firms of the map trade were aided in the mapping of North America by the endeavors of governmental agencies. Once the initial competition of the European powers faded and the geo-political outlines of North America were known, the secrecy of the early period no longer served a purpose. By the late eighteenth century the hydrographic offices of Spain, France, and Great Britain had all published charts of the water of the Gulf of Mexico, and these detailed charts were utilized as sources by the commercial map makers. In the nineteenth century the

A typical relief printing shop; from Diderot, *Encyclopédie*

United States Army, the several railroad and boundary surveys, the United States coast survey, and other government agencies like the General Land Office, were the most prolific generators of new information about the interior of the continent. The information gleaned from these official explorations was freely used by the commercial map makers to meet the seemingly insatiable demand of the public for more information about the world around them.

SPANISH CONQUESTS IN
"THE LAND OF AMERIGO"

Within scarcely more than a decade of the return of Columbus from his first voyage, various European powers followed up his initial discovery with numerous expeditions. Columbus himself made three additional treks probing the waters of the Gulf of Mexico and the Caribbean. John Cabot and the Corte Real brothers, Gaspar and Miguel, sailing respectively under English and Portuguese flags, made major discoveries along the northern coast of North America; Alonso de Ojeda and Juan de la Cosa extended knowledge of the northern coast of South America; and Pedro Alvarez Cabral previously had laid the Portuguese claim to Brazil. Perhaps the most important of these voyages, however, especially from the standpoint of adding geographical place names, was that undertaken by Amerigo Vespucci in 1501. Vespucci's account of that voyage, in which he claimed the discovery of the new world, achieved wide circulation and resulted in his name being assigned to the new continents. All of these discoveries began to appear in the printed world maps of the period, beginning with that of the Florentine geographer Giovanni Matteo Contarini in 1506. A great wall map by the cosmographer Martin Waldseemüller, published in St. Dié in northern France in 1507, was the first to attach Vespucci's name to the new lands. Most of the maps depicting the New World, however, appeared as supplements in the editions of Ptolemy's *Geography,* and perhaps the most important of these was the one published in Strassburg in 1513, with maps attributed to Waldseemüller. In addition to the standard twenty-seven maps of Ptolemy, this edition contained an appendix with twenty new maps. The cartographer presented on five of these maps the discoveries of the Spanish and the Portuguese, including one of the first printed maps to indicate the Gulf of Mexico (Plate 1).

The Spanish did not limit their advance to the islands of the Caribbean or to the northern coast of South America. In the first decade of the sixteenth century, Juan Ponce de Leon, whose quest for the elusive fountain of youth has been well known, reconnoitered the coasts of Florida. His pilot on these voyages, Anton de Alaminos, was later employed by Don Francisco de Garay to explore the territory that he had been granted on the North American mainland touching the Gulf of Mexico. Under the command of Alonso Alvarez de Piñeda, this expedition set sail from Puerto Rico in 1518 with Alaminos as pilot and explored the northern shore of the Gulf. They discovered the mouth of the Mississippi River, which they named the Espíritu Santo, and came into conflict with hostile natives along the Texas coast. Near the mouth of the Pánuco they were badly defeated, and many of the men were killed, including Piñeda. Only one ship escaped and sailed to the port of Vera Cruz. Despite the hardships and failures, the expedition of Piñeda was the first to explore the Texas coast, and the first to locate the Mississippi River. The report that bears Piñeda's name in the Archives of the Indies includes a crude but remarkably accurate sketch of the entire Gulf, the earliest known, on which it is clear that no passage existed to the Pacific.

The next expedition of discovery to contribute to the knowledge of the northern Gulf shore was that of Pánfilo de Narváez in 1527. Narváez received a grant from Charles V to conquer and colonize the vast territory along the Gulf between the Rio de las Palmas (now known as the Soto la Marina) and the Florida peninsula, and he mounted an expedition to lay claim to this grant. Narváez landed on the west coast of Florida and sent his ships to find a better anchorage to the west. Due to the hostility of the natives and the inhospitality of the climate and terrain, though, Narváez and his men failed to make the appointed rendezvous with the ships. Despite the fact that none of the men qualified as a shipwright, the intrepid explorers set about making rafts and set sail along the coast for Mexico. They floated past the mouth of the Mississippi but were overtaken by storms and shipwrecked somewhere on the Texas coast. Eventually all the men but four were lost to privation and the elements; most prominent of these survivors was Alvar Núñez Cabeza de Vaca, sergeant-at-arms of the expedition. He and his black companion, Estevánico, wandered among the Indians for almost eight years before finally making their way to Mexico, and in the process becoming the first Europeans to see much of the interior of the American Southwest. Cabeza de Vaca's narrative, first published in 1542, remains a cornerstone of discovery literature. His tales sparked great interest in the interior through which he had traveled, leading to the immediate explorations of Fray Marcos de Niza and eventually to the expedition of Francisco Vásquez de Coronado, who reconnoitered the territory as far as modern Kansas in his vain search for the Seven Cities of Cibola.

Another expedition inspired by the tales of Cabeza de Vaca had direct effect on the knowledge of Texas geography. Hernando de Soto, who was in Seville when Cabeza de Vaca arrived there from his experiences with the Indians, received a grant from Charles V, with an appointment as governor of Cuba and *adelantado* of Florida. De Soto landed in Florida in May 1539 and spent the next three years following the bad example of Pizzaro in Peru—antagonizing the natives. De Soto crossed the Mississippi in 1541 and proceeded as far west as the junction of the Canadian and Arkansas rivers in present-day Oklahoma before returning to the Mississippi, where he died from a fever on May 21, 1542. He was succeeded as adelantado by Luis Moscoso, who led another foray—perhaps as far as the upper Brazos—before returning to the Mississippi, constructing rafts, and sailing to Mexico in 1543.

The discoveries reported by Piñeda, Cabeza de Vaca, Coronado, de Soto and Moscoso were first codified into one map by the Spanish royal cosmographer, Alonso de Santa Cruz, in about 1544, a copy of which is preserved in the Archives of the Indies in Seville. It delineated the coast of the Gulf of Mexico from Tampico to Florida and gave the details of the interior as reported by explorers. Indian settlements in Texas such as Ays and Guasco appeared on a map for the first time with Santa Cruz's effort. This map was not available for commercial map makers to use for a source, however, and they were consequently forced to rely on rumor and innuendo for their information about the interior. This explains why the numerous editions of Ptolemy appearing during this period carried only crude maps of the New World, reflecting the meager information available.

The stark woodcut by Sebastian Münster (Plate 2) appearing in the 1540 Basel edition of Ptolemy and the attractive copperplate maps by Jacopo Gastaldi and Girolamo Ruscelli (Plate 3), which appeared in successive Venice editions of Ptolemy in 1548 and 1561 respectively, exemplified this lack of hard data. It was not until 1584, when Abraham Ortelius succeeded in enticing a map from another Spanish royal cosmographer, Geronimo Chaves, that accurate information on the explorations of the Spanish expeditions in the interior were printed on a map. First published in Ortelius's *Theatrum Orbis Terrarum* in 1584, the small map entitled *La Floride*, covering about the same territory as the Santa Cruz map forty years before, became the prototype which was copied by the map trade for several decades. It was reproduced as late as 1611 by Cornelius Wytfliet in his atlas of the new world (Plate 6). The only printed Spanish map of this period, appearing in Antonio de Herrera y Tordesillas's official *History of the Indies* in 1601 (Plate 7), is typical of the official Spanish secrecy concerning their domains: it reveals almost no information on the interior.

A PERIOD OF NEGLECT

Within forty years from Ponce de Leon's first sighting of Florida's west coast, then, the Gulf of Mexico and its hinterland had been explored and the hope of finding an interoceanic strait to the Orient at last abandoned. These discoveries did little to encourage further exploration by the Spanish in the area; on the contrary, they revealed that the interior of the continent directly north of the Gulf of Mexico held little interest to the Spanish, only hostile natives and still harsher climate and terrain. Their attention naturally turned elsewhere, to places where the investment of their energies and efforts might find a more ready return. After the expedition of Don Juan de Oñate to the upper Rio Grande revealed the existence of relatively more civilized natives, small Spanish excursions were directed to that quarter, where the Church's efforts to christianize the natives might be maximized. Texas was left virtually forgotten.

To the north during this same period, the French activity offered a marked contrast to the inattention of the Spanish. Following up the thrust of Cartier, who penetrated the St. Lawrence as early as 1534, the French fanned out through the rivers and lakes of the Northeast, establishing trading posts with the natives and exploring throughout the region. Such energetic figures as Marquette, Joliet, and Hennepin reported the results of their efforts to the official cartographer for maps of New France in the French Court, Jean Baptiste Louis Franquelin. By 1682 the French explorer René Robert Cavelier, Sieur de La Salle, had reconnoitered the Mississippi to its mouth and claimed the lands it drained for his king. Meanwhile, the British and the Dutch lost no time in establishing their own outposts and colonies on the Atlantic coast, and the French, British, and Spanish all came into conflict in the Southeast.

Throughout this period, despite the relative inactivity in the interior, the Gulf of Mexico itself was serving as a busy thoroughfare transporting the wealth of the Indies back to the coffers of the Spanish royal court. This traffic consequently generated great demand for nautical charts and sailing directions. The advances in the science of navigation brought corresponding advances in the charts used by mariners. These two developments were readily apparent in the seventeenth century publication by the Englishman Sir Robert Dudley, *Dell'Arcano del Mare* (The Secrets of the Sea). Published in Florence in 1646, it contained a series of beautifully engraved charts covering the entire world and definitive discussions of the science and instruments of navigation (Plate 9). During this same period the authority of Dutch chartmakers established earlier by Waghenaer was assumed by the house of Gerhard and Johan Van Keulen, who employed such leading scientists and mathematicians as Claes Jansz Vooght to contribute to their publications (Plate 11). The accuracy and comprehensiveness of their sea atlases were not seriously challenged throughout the second half of the seventeenth century. Meanwhile, the need of British seamen for navigational aids in their own language was served by *The English Pilot*, published by John Thornton and John Seller, and later by Richard Mount and Thomas Page. All of these productions revealed a steady increase in the knowledge of the Gulf coast.

The maps of the seventeenth century detailing the interior of North America, on the other hand, documented the progress of the French in Canada and the North, and the British along the Atlantic, but demonstrated clearly the lack of any real new information about the interior of that continent between the Rio Grande on the west and the Mississippi on the east. The map of North America appearing in the 1640 edition of Mercator's *Atlas*, published by his descendant Jan Jansson (Plate 8), depicted the explorations of Champlain in the north, but the Texas Gulf Coast showed few place names, with the interior covered by a fanciful interpretation of a buffalo.

The great French cartographer Nicolas Sanson produced a landmark map of North America in 1650, which contributed much new information on the Southwest, but was deficient in the Texas area. Perhaps the best indication of the knowledge of the interior geography was shown in the work of an official map maker to Louis XIV of France, the Italian Vincenzo Mario Coronelli. Drawing on the official sources of French explorers represented in the manuscript maps of Franquelin, Coronelli produced a series of maps and globes culminating in his *Atlante Veneto* in 1695. In most of these works Coronelli depicted the full course of the Mississippi, as explored by La Salle, but he placed its mouth hundreds of miles too far west, near the actual mouth of the Rio Grande (see Plate 12). The crude methods available at the time for estimating longitude caused this miscalculation, which similarly distorted the east-west dimensions of almost all maps. The error made in locating the mouth of the Mississippi set the stage for a serious confrontation in Texas.

THE FRENCH INTRUSION

After concluding his successful exploration of the Mississippi River, La Salle returned to France and secured permission to colonize at its mouth. The rationale for this undertaking, as set forth in La Salle's proposals, was not only to establish French control over the lands he had claimed, but also to serve as a base of attack on Spanish treasure ships in the Gulf, and the Spanish provinces around it, in the event of war.

La Salle set out from France in August 1684 with four ships and about three hundred colonists, arriving in the Gulf by the following January. Seeking the mouth of his great river too far west, La Salle made landfall near present Matagorda Bay, which he christened St. Louis, and established an armed camp. After seeking to establish friendly relations with the natives and to ascertain the location of Spanish presidios, La Salle made a number of abortive attempts to locate the Mississippi. The failure of these attempts, coupled with the increasing hostility of the Indians and the loss of his ships, convinced La Salle that he needed assistance either from France or from Frenchmen in the colonies. He decided that Canada, reached by way of the Mississippi, was his best chance for aid, and he set off again in search of the river in January 1687. Along the way his men murdered him, possibly in the vicinity of present Navasota, Texas. With his death the leadership of the venture fell to Henri Joutel, who in 1688 led a few survivors out of the wilderness and eventually back to France. Those colonists left in Texas all perished save for a few children eventually found by the Spanish. Although failing in its purposes, La Salle's expedition nevertheless had a lasting impact on the development of Texas: it forced the Spanish to turn their attention there in order to erect a barrier to further French encroachment in the Gulf area.

Rumors of the French intrusion reached Mexico not long after La Salle's arrival on the coast, and the Spanish authorities immediately reacted. Numerous attempts were made by sea to find the colony, and although they succeeded in locating the wreckage of French ships on the coast, the settlement itself remained undetected. Despairing of that approach, the Spanish viceroy in 1686 ordered an expedition of fifty men under the leadership of Captain Alonso de Leon to locate the French colony. Over the next five years de Leon made five expeditions to Texas. It was on the fourth of these, in the spring of 1689, that de Leon, then serving as Governor of Coahuila, finally located Fort St. Louis, which had been destroyed. The following year de Leon made his last trip to Texas, in the company of Father Demian Massanet, for the purpose of establishing a permanent mission in Texas to serve as a deterrent to further French aggression. They reconnoitered East Texas and established San Francisco de las Tejas on the Neches River. This marked the beginning of the Spanish missionary and colonial enterprise in Texas, which was to last for more than a century and indelibly stamp a Spanish character on the heritage of Texas.

Maps of the period began to reflect the first-hand knowledge of Texas garnered from the La Salle venture and the Spanish response it produced. The French engineer Minet, who accompanied La Salle, made a sketch of their landing place on Matagorda Bay and transmitted it to the French geographer Franquelin. Copies of Minet's maps found their way into the hands of Pedro de Ronquillo, Spanish ambassador to England, and from there to the Spanish authorities, who preserved them in the Archives of the Indies in Seville. Most important, however, from the standpoint of a lasting effect on Texas cartography, were the maps resulting from the numerous treks of Alonso de Leon. De Leon, as the first Spanish official to traverse much of this territory, appended names to many features for the first time, and he compounded the existing confusion over the location of the Mississippi River by christening Matagorda Bay and the Colorado River both with the name Espíritu Santo, a name which had been applied a century before to the Mississippi. Printed maps of the period also reflected La Salle's explorations. The French geographer Nicolas de Fer added a delicate and attractive map (see Color Plate II; also Plate 13) depicting La Salle's exploits to his popular atlas, and Henri Joutel published his journal of the expedition, including a map depicting the theater for the expedition.

SPANISH COLONIZATION

The La Salle-de Leon episode was merely the first act in a drama that unfolded for the better part of a century as Spain and France confronted each other on the frontiers of their respective claims. For a time there was a respite, however, and the mission established in 1689 by de Leon and Massanet was abandoned by 1693 because of the increasing hostility of the natives and the immense logistical problem of supplying an outpost so far from the settlements in northern Mexico. Perhaps the primary factor in the abandonment, however, was that the Spanish found no Frenchmen in the area.

In the meantime, the French had continued to explore and exploit their province of Louisiana. Jean Baptiste Le Moyne, Sieur d'Bienville and his brother Pierre, Sieur d'Iberville, received a royal patent to colonize Louisiana in 1698, and they spent the next ten years probing the Gulf coast and the interior as far as the Red River. They realized the potential benefit of trade with the Spanish and the Indians of the territory to the west and one of their lieutenants, Louis Juchereau de St. Denis, was commissioned in 1713 to open an overland route. In 1714 St. Denis crossed Texas from Louisiana to the nearest Spanish outpost at the presidio and mission of San Juan Bautista on the Rio Grande where he fostered good relations and established important connections with the Spanish. St. Denis returned to Texas in the spring of 1716 as the guide to the expedition of Domingo Ramón, who, with St. Denis's active assistance, established six missions and a presidio in East Texas. The French encouraged this venture because it seemed inevitable that the new missions would depend heavily on the nearby French in Louisiana for trade. In an effort to counteract this tendency and to improve communications with the eastern mission, the governor of Coahuila, Martín de Alarcón, provided for a half-way post between them and the Rio Grande. For this purpose the mission of San Antonio de Valero was established in 1718, at a location destined to become the most important Spanish post in Texas, San Antonio de Béxar.

In 1719, following a conflict between Spain and France, the East Texas missions were once again briefly abandoned, but in 1721 the viceroy commanded the Marquis de San Miguel de Aguayo to lead a major force into East Texas and to re-establish Spanish control permanently. Aguayo, as governor and captain-general of Coahuila and Texas, relocated the missions and increased their number to nine, manned and provisioned four presidios, secured two civil settlements, and designated Los Adaes as capital. Aguayo's efforts marked the apogee of Spanish occupation in the eighteenth century. He was followed shortly by Pedro de Rivera y Villalon, who was commissioned to reduce government expenditures and whose recommendations resulted in the relocation of several missions in 1730. Most important, however, Rivera set out to explore systematically and to map the territory. His logical insistence upon learning more about the territory before deciding how it should be structured and governed produced the first attempt to define accurately the geography of Texas.

The Spanish continued to be motivated by fear and by the suspicion of French and British designs on their territory. An examination of the coast of the Gulf of Mexico revealed that between Tampico and the French settlements in Louisiana not a single Spanish establishment guarded their interests; they set out to remedy that in 1747. In that year the Spanish created the province of Nuevo Santander astride the lower Rio Grande and commissioned José de Escandón, a brilliant career military officer, as its governor-general. During the next several years they erected numerous settlements in the region, including Comargo, Reynosa, Mier, and Laredo. The boundaries of the province extended as far north as the San Antonio River, and this was to have lasting effect on the political geography of Texas.

In 1748 the Spanish established the mission of San Gabriel to the northeast of San Antonio to minister to the Tonkawa Indians and in 1756 they built the mission of San Sabá to the northwest of San Antonio to minister to the Apaches. In 1755 a French trader was arrested in southeast Texas, an occasion which promoted the establishment of a mission and presidio the following year near the site of present-day Liberty. Ostensibly founded to convert the Orcoquisac Indians, the principal purpose of the settlement was in reality to reinforce the strategic defense of East Texas from coastal approaches.

Perhaps the final episode of the Franco-Spanish rivalry in the Texas region occurred in 1759 when Diego Ortiz Parrilla led a punitive expedition from San Antonio against marauding Comanches. Parrilla's massive force pursued the Indians as far as the Red River where, to the amazement of the Spanish, stood a fortified town flying the French flag and armed with French guns. Parrilla charged the fort but was routed by the Comanches and fled back to Béxar. The town they had found was the center of Indian commerce for French traders, who had supplied them arms and ammunition. The site was eventually abandoned by the French, and later by the Indians, and when encountered by Anglo pioneer settlers in the next century who knew nothing of its history, it was dubbed Spanish Fort.

In the 1760s European affairs once again dominated the events of discovery in the New World. The Seven Years' War (known in America as the French and Indian War) began drawing to a close when the French realized that they were beaten. To prevent Louisiana from falling into British hands, France ceded it to Spain by the Treaty of Fontainebleau in 1762. The transfer was confirmed by the Treaty of Paris the following year. This concluded the war, and a Spanish government was established in New Orleans. The Treaty of Paris not only closed the curtain on the last act of the century-long conflict for empire between Spain and France, but also made Britain and Spain neighbors along the entire length of the Mississippi. It thus rendered obsolete the East Texas missions as a buffer against the French in Louisiana. In 1764 retrenchment began under the Marquis de Rubí who made an inspection of the province in that year. His recommendations were incorporated in a royal decree known as the New Regulations for the Presidios of the Frontier, promulgated in 1772. The decree closed several missions and moved the capital of Texas to San Antonio; the East Texas missions were abandoned. Having survived the French threat to her territory, Spain turned to face a far more aggressive British opponent across the Mississippi.

The exploration of Texas occasioned by the French and Spanish confrontation naturally resulted in new maps of the territory. All of the many Spanish expeditions and inspections resulted in reports and at least a manuscript sketch map, many of which were deposited in the Archives of the Indies. The earliest report, after those of de Leon and others searching for La Salle, was that of the viceroy's legal counsel (*auditor*) Don Juan de Oliván Robolledo, submitted in 1717. The map it transmitted was remarkable for its lack of detail, giving only a vague impression of Texas as a land watered by a plethora of streams. The expedition of the Marquis de San Miguel de Aguayo resulted in numerous sketches and plans, primarily of the missions and pueblos established by the Marquis. Not until the expedition of Rivera in 1727 did the Spanish attempt any systematic mapping of the province. Rivera was accompanied by a talented young engineer, Francisco Alvarez Barriero, who had served as a military engineer in Texas under Aguayo from 1717 to 1720. Barriero's maps of the province mark the first renderings of Texas by a trained cartographer from his own observations. They stood unsurpassed for forty years, until Nicolás de La Fora and José de Urritia prepared a map to accompany the report of the Marquis de Rubí. Urritia also prepared numerous sketches and plats of the missions and presidios to accompany the report.

These firsthand Spanish reports were almost certainly unavailable to the map trade. Nonetheless, because of European interest in this conflict, the output of printed maps of America increased tremendously, and most of these relied on French sources. The great French cartographer Guillaume Delisle had access to the official French documents, and his maps reveal the influence of this information. His 1703 map of Mexico and Florida (see Color Plate III; also Plate 14) referred to the explorations of d'Iberville explicitly, which his landmark map of Louisiana of 1718 (Plate 19) revealed the wide geographic knowledge of the French sources of the area, detailing the track of St. Denis scarcely two years after his journey across Texas. Delisle's maps were copied assiduously by map makers throughout Europe, and map sellers like Herman Moll, John Senex, Matthew Seutter, Peter Schenk, and Johann Baptiste Homann all issued editions of Delisle's American maps (see Plates 16–18). The accuracy and reliability of Delisle's work is attested by comparing the 1718 map with the one made the year before by Robolledo, revealing the remarkable inferiority of the Spanish knowledge of their own territory, which is further documented by the only printed Spanish map of the period, that of North America prepared by the mathematician and scientist José Antonio de Alzate y Ramirez in 1768 (Plate 20). He badly distorted the geography of Texas, giving poor details, and completely omitting the Brazos River. It was only through the maps of Delisle, a half century earlier, that Texas began to take shape recognizable to the modern eye.

THE AMERICAN CHALLENGE

After 1763 the British, although positioned to challenge the Spanish in Louisiana, were far too occupied with the internal problems of their own colonial empire. Just twenty years after the Treaty of Paris another treaty of the same name was enacted to end the American Revolution, establishing the new American Republic as Spain's neighbor across the Mississippi. During that same twenty year period Spain had been occupied with the internal reorganization of her own empire, as recommended by the Marquis de Rubí. One of the primary features of this reorganization was the creation of the *Provincias Internas*, in which the northern provinces of New Spain were removed from the control of the viceroy and their commandant reported directly to Spain. They also inaugurated a new policy toward the Indians, predicated on an attempt to ally the northern tribes with the Spanish against the Lipan Apaches. The success of this policy relied on the activities of a number of Frenchmen with wide frontier experience who had remained in Louisiana with the change of administrations. One of these was Pedro Vial.

Vial was commissioned to explore a route between San Antonio and Santa Fe in 1786, when he left San Antonio with a Comanche band, arriving in Santa Fe in May 1787. The following year he reconnoitered a route from Santa Fe to Natchitoches, following the Red River from its headwaters, and returned to Santa Fe via San Antonio the following year. Vial made careful observations and kept detailed records of the rivers and streams, as well as other significant topographical features, and he submitted a complete report of his ventures, which included several maps. Vial later opened direct communication between Santa Fe and Saint Louis and was actively trading with the Indians from his Santa Fe base as late as 1803.

During this period the Spanish hydrographic office had been conducting detailed surveys of the coast of the Gulf of Mexico and in 1799 it published the first reasonably accurate marine chart of that body of water, the *Carta Esférica* (see Plate 22A).

This chart superceded the map of the coast of Texas by the prominent British cartographer Thomas Jefferys (Plate 21), which had served as a model for almost twenty-five years.

At the turn of the eighteenth century, developments in Europe once again intervened in explorations in the Americas. Under pressure from Napoleon, Spain ceded Louisiana back to France in 1800 in the Treaty of San Ildefonso. Three short years later, hard pressed in Haiti and requiring funds for his ventures elsewhere, Napoleon was forced to abandon his dreams of a New World empire; he sold Louisiana to the United States for sixty million francs. On December 20, 1803, Louisiana was officially transferred to the United States, and the Spanish officials found themselves in an even worse dilemma than before.

The western boundary of Louisiana had never been defined. When Spain acquired it in 1763, it adjoined her other North American possessions, and when it was returned to France in 1800, the treaty merely specified that it had the same boundary as when it had originally been ceded by the French. The United States acquired this same vague line, and with it, all of France's old claims in North America. Napoleon, far from being concerned with the boundary problem, reportedly said that if no ambiguity had existed, it would have been wise to create one. In any event, many in the United States, including President Jefferson, considered Louisiana to extend at least as far southwest as La Salle's Fort Saint Louis, and some thought to the Rio Grande. The precise location of the boundary remained to be settled by direct negotiations between the United States and Spain.

In the meantime, Jefferson immediately began to probe the area to determine the nature of the land and its people. He sent out numerous expeditions, including those of the well-known adventurers Lewis and Clark to the upper Missouri, Thomas Freeman to the headwaters of the Red River, and Captain Zebulon Montgomery Pike to the Arkansas. Spanish officials viewed with trepidation and alarm these expeditions, as well as the independent influx of American frontiersmen. As early as 1790 Spain had felt the aggressive American thrust when Philip Nolan, with the connivance of Major General James Wilkinson of the United States Army, had begun horse-trading forays into Texas. Nolan was killed in 1801 while resisting a Spanish force sent to arrest him, but Wilkinson, who was given command of all United States troops in the South in 1800, was involved in schemes concerning Texas for the next twenty years. The most interesting of these occurred in 1806 when Aaron Burr, after lengthy conferences with Wilkinson, led an armed party of men down the Mississippi; his intentions are subject to much speculation. Denounced by Wilkinson after a warrant for his arrest had been issued, Burr was tried for treason but convicted on a lesser charge. Just precisely what Wilkinson and his associates Nolan and Burr were attempting has remained shrouded in mystery, but the effect of this incident on the Spaniards was clear. Shortly after the American occupation of New Orleans at the transfer of governments, Spain re-garrisoned the old East Texas presidios of Orcoquisac and Los Adaes. Spanish expeditions were sent out, turning back Freeman near the present boundary of Arkansas, and arresting Pike in the vicinity of Santa Fe. War between the United States and Spain seemed imminent, and was avoided only by an unofficial agreement between Wilkinson and his Spanish counterpart, Simón de Herrera. Known as the Neutral Ground Agreement, this codicil stipulated that American forces would remain east of the Aroyo Hondo, a stream in western Louisiana, while the Spanish would stay west of the Sabine, pending the establishment of the boundary through diplomatic channels. The agreement was scrupulously honored by both sides for a number of years.

Although this lessened the immediate threat of war along the eastern boundary, the Spanish were still concerned that Americans were stirring up trouble with the Comanches. In 1808

Francisco Amangual made what was to be the last Spanish expedition in the Southwest to distribute presents to the Comanches and renew their pledges of loyalty. Amangual set out from San Antonio with five companies of soldiers and crossed the high plains via the old presidio at San Sabá, arriving in Santa Fe near the end of the year. He returned to San Antonio along the Pecos in 1809. Despite the fact that he found no evidence that Americans were fomenting difficulties with the Indians, his report did little to allay the fears of Spanish officials. It included an interesting map detailing his route.

Three other manuscript contributions to the cartography of the period deserve mention. The first of these is a large map drawn in 1805 by a Louisiana-born engineer serving in the Spanish army in Mexico, Juan Pedro Walker. Although it covers virtually all of the Spanish Southwest, the detail it shows in Texas is remarkable, particularly in its depiction of the course of the Colorado River. Two manuscript copies of this map are now known, one in the Huntington Library and one in the Barker Texas History Center at The University of Texas at Austin.

The second map was drawn about 1807 by Father José Maria Puelles, a Franciscan friar then stationed in Nacogdoches. Puelles compiled an excellent rendering of the known inland features of Texas, and although his depiction of the coast was deficient, his view of the rivers represented a significant advance. He was probably the first to properly locate the Brazos and to indicate its size and course.

In 1808, preparing for the difficult negotiations with the United States over the western boundary of Louisiana, the Spanish government commissioned a Mexican friar, José Antonio Pichardo, to compile all the pertinent data. Pichardo, a scholar of wide background in the classics and the sciences, spent four years studying the voluminous records he had at his disposal. His report, issued in 1812, was a compendium of all the relevant data concerning the Texas-Louisiana border and included a large map that included the explorations and the settlements of Spain in the province.

A noteworthy turning point in the cartographic history of Texas occurred in 1810, when three separate maps were published bringing the area into new focus. During the first few years of the nineteenth century the great European savant, Alexander von Humboldt, had been a guest of the Spanish government in Mexico, studying the natural history of the country. His semi-official status provided him access to many confidential sources, and among the works his stay produced was a large map of New Spain. Although he left Mexico in 1804, the map was not published until 1810, when it appeared with his *Political Essay on the Kingdom of New Spain* (Plate 23). In the meantime, Zebulon Pike had been escorted back to the United States across Texas, and in 1810 he published a report on his own adventures, including a map (Plate 24). In that same year the great British map maker Aaron Arrowsmith published a large map of Mexico (Plate 25). Humboldt publicly denounced both the Pike and the Arrowsmith works as copies of his own. Who copied from whom is difficult to determine, but taken together the three maps mark a genuine advance in the geography of the region.

Also occurring in 1810 was the first significant internal threat against Spain's control of Mexico—the Hidalgo Revolt. Led by a parish priest, Miguel Hidalgo y Costilla, the revolt organized those who were deeply concerned about the plight of the masses of poor in Mexico, as contrasted with the wealth of Spain. Although it was easily put down, it marked the beginning of a series of such disorders during the next several years. In the next few years the Spanish officials in Mexico began to feel a mounting pressure from the east in the form of filibusters seeking to capitalize on the unsettled political conditions. In 1813 Bernardo Gutierrez de Lara, an associate of Hidalgo, persuaded an American army lieutenant, Augustus W. Magee, to resign his commission and command an expedition to foment revolt in Texas. Although he succeeded in capturing San Antonio, he was ultimately defeated. This threat was followed in the decade, however, by similar invasions by forces commanded by Luis Aury and Francisco Mina.

Outside intervention in Texas was spurred by the final diplomatic settlement of the boundary problem between Spain and the United States in the form of the Adams-Oñis Treaty in 1819. To secure Spanish concessions in Florida, the American minister, John Quincy Adams, accepted a delineation of the Louisiana boundary well to the east of the United States's claim. The boundary followed what are now the eastern and northern boundaries of Texas, and were perhaps first delineated on a map published in 1819 by John Hamilton Robinson (Plate 27), who had been an associate of Pike's and later a general in the Mexican Army. This compromise surrendered territory that many Americans believed to be rightfully a part of Louisiana, and it set off a spate of attempts to "restore" Texas to the United States. Perhaps most notable of these was that of James Long, who was elected at a vehement protest meeting in Natchez, Mississippi, to lead a group of volunteers. Long (whose wife was a niece of General James Wilkinson) and his associates were deluded into thinking that the people of Texas were ripe to rebel against the yoke of Spain and would quickly join their cause. After an abortive raid on Nacogdoches, Long regrouped at New Orleans, then at Galveston, before landing near La Bahía in October 1821. The presidio fell quickly, but was just as quickly retaken when a royalist army arrived on the scene. Long and his men were captured and taken to Mexico, where he was shot some months later.

The boundary of Louisiana stipulated by the Adams-Oñis Treaty was both controversial and difficult to locate. Although the treaty precisely defined the boundary as following the Sabine River to the thirty-second parallel, no one knew with any assurance where that line intersected the course of this stream. In reality, the Sabine makes a sweeping curve to the west just north of the thirty-second parallel. This curve was displaced to the south and greatly exaggerated on Melish's map (Plate 26), on which the treaty line had been set down. As a result, much territory actually in Texas was thought to be in the southwest corner of Arkansas. In 1820 the Arkansas legislature duly created Miller County in its southwestern corner and opened it for settlement. Miller County soon had a population of hundreds, most located in the settlements of Pecan Point and Jonesborough. It was years before the boundary was settled, and as late as 1834 a Mexican official visiting there had to assure the population that they would be issued legal titles to their land by the government of Mexico if Miller County indeed proved to be part of Texas. The ambiguity of this situation, caused in effect by the inaccuracy of Melish's map, is epitomized by the fact that while Richard Ellis was representing the county in the Texas Convention of 1836, his son was representing the same county in the Arkansas Legislature.

ANGLO COLONIZATION

In 1821 a new chapter in the history of the American Southwest opened when Moses Austin, a bankrupt lead miner and merchant living in Potosi in Spanish Missouri, secured permission from the governor of Texas to introduce 300 American families into Texas. Austin died shortly after the grant, but his son, Stephen Fuller Austin, inherited the father's enterprise and by the end of 1821 had located several families on the Colorado near Columbus and at Washington-on-the-Brazos. Before he was able to proceed further, however, Austin's colonizing effort received a severe setback. Mexico successfully revolted against Spain in 1821 and declared itself independent. The governor informed Austin that his colony had been granted by Spain but was not recognized by the new government.

In April 1822, Austin journeyed to Mexico City seeking confirmation of his grant. Because of the unsettled political situation in the capital, which resulted in a succession of revolving-door governments, he was forced to spend nearly a year there. During this period he made the acquaintance of a number of influential Mexican politicians and came into contact with many of the ambitious foreigners who had flooded the capital upon independence seeking permission from the government to speculate in the unoccupied lands of Texas. While he was in Mexico he drew a map of the province, based on a copy of Puelles's map that had come into his possession, to which he added information from the limited surveying accomplished in Texas prior to his departure. He distributed several copies of this map to his associates, and probably included copies of it in his petitions to the successive governments that deliberated his case. In these petitions Austin promised to improve the map and eventually provide the government with an accurate depiction of the entire province if his grant were confirmed. Finally, in April 1823, Austin received a special contract with the government confirming his license to settle 300 families in central Texas. He immediately returned to Texas and began to issue titles to his colonists as quickly as the claims could be surveyed. By the end of the following summer he had settled 272 of the allotted 300 families.

Austin was not the only empressario to be granted a colonization contract. The Federal Colonization Law of 1824 delegated to the several Mexican states the responsibility for overseeing the colonization of their lands, and in March 1825 the State of Coahuila y Texas passed its own act. Under its authority grants were shortly made with several individuals, among them Haden Edwards, Green C. DeWitt, Martin de Leon, and Robert Leftwich, an agent for the Texas Association of Nashville. Austin was also given three additional contracts. These empressarios were so successful in attracting Americans to Texas that by 1828 Mexican officials came to be alarmed that Texas was becoming completely Americanized. Manuel de Mier y Terán was sent to investigate these new conditions, as well as to survey the eastern boundary of Texas.

Terán entered Texas at Laredo in February 1828 and made his way slowly across it, reaching Nacogdoches in June. His expedition included such notable scientists as Jean Louis Berlandier, and the party made many astronomical and other scientific observations as they went. Terán recorded his geographical observations as corrections to a map in his possession, which had been lithographed in Mexico in 1826 (Plate 28). This rather crude map claims the distinction of being the first printed map showing Texas as a separate entity.

Terán noted that Mexican influence decreased markedly as he moved northeast, and was alarmed to find Nacogdoches thoroughly Americanized, even having an English-speaking school. He feared that, if allowed to go unchecked, the Americanization of Texas could have disastrous consequences for Mexico, and his report contained a series of recommendations for extending Mexican control over the province. These recommendations were extended by the new centralist regime in Mexico and incorporated into the Law of April 6, 1830, which established Mexican garrisons across Texas and prohibited further immigration of Americans. The colonists resented these provisions, and their reaction to the law represented the beginnings of sentiment that eventually resulted in war.

Throughout this period Austin continued his map making endeavors as he had promised in his petitions. As a consequence of establishing settlers and surveying their grants, Austin came into possession of the most up-to-date and detailed information available. He also sought additional information from other empressarios, colonists, and explorers. Commissioned by the Mexican government to chart Galveston Bay in 1826, Austin prepared several detailed maps for special purposes, such as a military campaign against the Comanches. He met and became close friends with Terán, despite their differing views of Anglo colonization, and this relationship was the source of much additional detailed information. By 1829 Austin had completed his large map of Texas. He sent copies of it to several government officials and, more important, he arranged to have it published by H. S. Tanner, the prominent map publisher in Philadelphia (see Color Plate IV; also Plate 29). Austin viewed his map not only as an appropriate activity for a civic-minded citizen and a politically expedient gift to the Mexican government, but also as an effective instrument for subtly advertising Texas in a way that would not alarm the Mexicans.

The map trade in the 1820s had taken notice of the enormous interest in Texas and had begun to supply maps catering to it. In 1827 Phillipe van der Maelen's *Atlas Universel*, the most lavish and detailed cartographic production of the decade and the first major lithographed atlas, included five maps depicting parts of Texas. These maps were based primarily on the outmoded models of Humboldt and Pike and contributed no new knowledge. The British publisher Sidney Hall, on the other hand, in 1828 published a map of Mexico "corrected from original infor-

mation communicated by Simon A. G. Bourne, Esq." Bourne was an associate of James Long, Arthur Wavell, and Benajmin Milam, all of whom had special interests in Texas land. He spent several years in Mexico and Texas, had a copy of Austin's 1822 map, and wrote a brief description of Texas published in 1828. Hall's map revealed this firsthand knowledge in its depiction of Texas's rivers and settlements.

In 1825 H. S. Tanner published a large map of Mexico giving detailed information of the area. This map was copied in 1828 by the firm White, Gallaher, and White (Plate 37), with no credit to Tanner. In 1833 David H. Burr, later geographer to the U.S. House of Representatives, published the first large-scale map of Texas to include the present-day panhandle (see Color Plate V; also Plate 30). Burr's map was copied by J. H. Young in 1835 and included an inset of Galveston Bay by Alexander Thompson, which was the first accurate printed map of that important port. In 1833, Austin's cousin Mary Austin Holley produced a promotional tract on Texas which, because Tanner refused Austin permission to use his map for the purpose, was issued with an accompanying map by William Hooker, which was clearly based on Austin's sources. Austin was not the only empressario to see the promotional value of maps; both the Colorado and Red River Land Company and the Galveston Bay and Texas Land Company published maps depicting their grants and extolling the virtues of their land.

The Law of April 6, 1830, did not end colonization entirely; it only banned American colonists. Many enterprises introducing colonists from Europe were established in the following years. The first of these was a colony of Irish Catholics under the leadership of John McMullen and his son-in-law James McGloin, who in 1831 founded the town of San Patricio on the Nueces River near Corpus Christi Bay. They were followed in 1833 by another group of Irishmen under James Power and James Hewetson, who located between the Lavaca and the Guadalupe rivers. Other empressarios awarded grants after 1830 included John Charles Beales, Joseph Vehlein, David G. Burnet, and Lorenzo de Zavala. The last three of these held grants in southeast Texas, which came to be administered by the Galveston Bay and Texas Land Company.

REVOLUTION AND REPUBLIC

During the 1830s political upheaval in Mexico—resulting from a continuing struggle for supremacy between the federalist and centralists, and, exacerbated by the machinations of a few ambitious individuals—led to uncertainty and unrest among the colonists of Texas. Texans favored the federalist cause, then championed by Antonio López de Santa Anna. When Santa Anna was elected president of the republic in 1832, the Texans hoped for better relations with the government. Their rising optimism soon vanished, however, as Santa Anna gradually revealed himself to be a cynical opportunist. He soon dissolved the congress and abrogated the constitution. In successive conventions in 1832, 1833, 1835, and 1836, Texans produced increasingly radical petitions and resolutions, beginning with a cautious request for a repeal of the Law of April 6, 1830, then progressing through petitions for separate statehood and a restoration of the constitution of 1824, and finally culminating in an outright declaration of independence. The brief military campaign of 1836 ended in the decisive defeat of Santa Anna at San Jacinto.

Having won its independence on the battlefield, Texas was then faced with the problems of establishing a stable government, defending its borders, and receiving international recognition; however, its most pressing problem was to gain a strong fiscal base. The republic had to finance its enormous debt, incurred during the revolution and increased by its continuing defense operations. To accomplish this, it turned to the one commodity of which it had a surplus—land. In 1841 the congress authorized a grant to a group of investors from Louisville headed by W. S. Peters. First known as the Peters Colony, the group underwent a series of reorganizations and emerged finally as the Texas Emigration and Land Company, with a grant of ten thousand square miles on the Red River. Dallas was established in the colony in 1842 and the company claimed to have settled 2,300 families in the next six years. The new congress passed a general colonization

law in 1842 and several other colonies were chartered under its provisions. They included the Mercer Colony southeast of the Peters Colony, the Castro Colony west of San Antonio, and the German colonies under the *Adelsverein* in a three million acre reserve west and south of Austin. These ventures helped to increase population to the republic, added to its social and cultural diversity, and pushed the frontier line farther and farther west.

Defense of the republic from the twofold threat of Indian depredations and Mexican invasions became a primary concern of each successive administration. Indian raids were not restricted to the isolated homesteads on the western frontier. In August 1840, for example, a band of Comanches ravaged the town of Victoria. The primary defense against these attacks were the frontier regiments of the Texas Rangers and strong local militia companies. In 1837 President Sam Houston established a string of blockhouse forts along the edge of the frontier, which at that time paralleled the coast and ran from just west of San Antonio to the Sabine River north of Nacogdoches. The punitive expeditions against the Indians that sallied forth from this primitive line of defense contributed greatly to a developing conception of Texas geography.

Relations with Mexico presented a more intractable defense problem, compounded by the instability of Mexican governments and the recalcitrance of their demands. The Mexican refusal to recognize Texas's independence left the borders between the two republics unsettled. Texas claimed the Rio Grande as its border, from its mouth to its headwaters, and in the spring of 1841 President Mirabeau B. Lamar sent an expedition to Santa Fe to divert its trade to the Texas coast and to establish Texas political jurisdiction there. Apparently none of the 300 men who set out from San Antonio that June were familiar with their route, and they wandered about on the High Plains for some time. When they finally stumbled into New Mexico, they were immediately captured, marched off to Mexico, and incarcerated in Perote

Castle. The hardships and privations of these men were chronicled by George Wilkins Kendall, New Orleans journalist, and the British writer Thomas Falconer, both of whom were with the expedition. Maps were included in both of these publications (Plate 34) and probably exposed their readers to the geography of the Santa Fe area for the first time.

The Santa Fe expedition accomplished nothing for Texas except to provoke Santa Anna, who was then back in power, into an invasion of Texas. The Mexican forces under General Adrian Woll succeeded in taking San Antonio and holding it for a brief time. In retaliation, the Texans sent an ill-prepared foray against the town of Mier across the Rio Grande, which only resulted in the addition of 176 men to the group of prisoners in Perote. Even when Santa Anna was again overthrown in 1844, Mexico still refused to recognize Texas.

The Republic period, with its large influx of colonists and its many military expeditions against the Indians and the Mexicans, resulted in an almost exponential increase in the knowledge of the interior of Texas. Even before the revolution was won, the American map publisher T. G. Bradford added a new, separate map of Texas to his 1835 atlas (Plate 31); he also incorporated an improved version into his 1838 atlas as well. Many of the maps produced during this period were clearly published for promotional purposes, depicting the various grants and surveys and highlighting the land available to settlers. Typical of this genre was the map which accompanied Hunt and Randel's semiofficial *Guide to the Republic of Texas*. John Arrowsmith, the well-known kinsman of British cartographer Aaron Arrowsmith, produced a map that appeared in several forms in 1841 (Plate

32), including the laudatory book by British Chargé d'Affairs William Kennedy. In addition to these maps appearing in books and atlases, a number of maps of Texas were issued separately during this period, including productions of such well-known publishers as James Wyld, J. H. Young, S. A. Mitchell, and H. S. Tanner.

One of the most valuable sources of information for these commercial map makers were the various official surveys and explorations undertaken by government groups. Hunt and Randel, for example, relied heavily on the records of the General Land Office for primary information. One of the most important of these official productions during the Republic was the publication in 1842 of the report of the Joint United States-Texas Boundary Commission, which for the first time depicted the eastern border of Texas from Sabine Lake to the Red River, thus settling at last the problem of Miller County. In addition, the British, French, and Mexican hydrographic offices all produced charts during this time, and they were utilized by the important chart-printing firm of E. and G. W. Blunt in making their large chart of the coast published in 1837. Finally, as the Republic period drew to a close, the United States Army saw the likelihood of a future war in the Texas region and, planning for that contingency, produced a landmark map (Plate 33). Compiled by William H. Emory of the Corps of Topographical Engineers, for whom this was merely the beginning of a long association with Texas and the Southwest, the map represented the best available topographical description of the region at the time of its publication in 1844.

A NEW AMERICAN STATE

In the first general election held in the Republic of Texas in September 1836, the voters not only ratified a new constitution and elected officers and representatives, but they also voted overwhelmingly in favor of annexing Texas to the United States. This goal, though, was frustrated for almost a decade by the internal politics of the United States as well as by the changing moods and needs of the Texans. Finally the United States, alarmed by the potential British influence in Texas and at the prospect of a British satellite on their frontier, took action. After a false start in 1844, a treaty of annexation was finally concluded in 1845, with terms admitting Texas directly as a state and allowing her to keep her public lands. This move by the United States was viewed as a hostile act by Mexico, which still claimed Texas. In May 1846, Mexican troops crossed the Rio Grande, which they did not acknowledge as an international boundary, and attacked an American regiment under Gen. Zachary Taylor. The U.S.-Mexican War, thus begun, resulted in the American invasion and occupation of Mexico. It ended with the Treaty of Guadalupe-Hidalgo, signed by American and Mexican plenipotentiaries, in February 1848.

Public awareness of the addition of the new state of Texas, as well as of the general westward expansion of the United States, was aided by map publisher Samuel Augustus Mitchell (see Color Plate VI; also Plate 36). His map became especially popular following the outbreak of the Mexican-American War. During the war, the various troop movements and invasions—not only in Texas and Mexico but throughout the southwest in New Mexico, Arizona, and California—added significantly to the knowledge of the terrain in those regions. Each expedition made careful observations, took copious notes, and issued detailed reports containing maps. William H. Emory, for example, was attached to the expedition, commanded by Stephen W. Kearny, which marched from Fort Leavenworth, Kansas, through Santa Fe and New Mexico, to California. Emory kept a journal and constructed a map at the conclusion of the march based on his own and other engineers' observations. The resulting document represents the first scientific mapping of the entire region based on actual observation. After the war the army continued to be one of the primary agencies of exploration in the newly won territories.

In the Treaty of Guadalupe-Hidalgo, Mexico recognized the Rio Grande as the boundary of Texas and ceded all the occupied territories west of the river to the United States. Accordingly, the treaty seemed to reinforce the Texas claim to the upper Rio Grande and eastern New Mexico. Acting on this assumption, the Texas Legislature on March 15, 1848, duly created Santa Fe County and sent an emissary west to organize the county and establish control. The people of Santa Fe and New Mexico rejected the emissary, along with the idea of Texas's authority in the region. Instead they held a constitutional convention, and petitioned Congress for separate admission to the Union, claiming in the process a large portion of Texas. The problem of the boundary between Texas and New Mexico thus became a federal matter and was settled as a part of the Compromise of 1850. In return for the assumption of its public debt by the federal government, Texas relinquished its claim to New Mexico and agreed to the present boundaries. These boundaries were surveyed by the surveyor general of the United States in 1859 and 1860, and finally ratified by all parties in 1896.

One further key provision of the Treaty of Guadalupe-Hidalgo was to have great impact on the cartographic history of the Southwest. Article V of the document defined the boundary between the two republics, stipulating that the southern and western limits of New Mexico should be those laid down in Disturnell's map of 1847 (see Color Plate VII; Plate 38). The article also provided for the establishment of a bilateral boundary commission to survey and mark the border. This seemingly simple task became complicated because the Disturnell map, like the Melish treaty map thirty years earlier, had several major errors or distortions, and the result was a technical and diplomatic furor that took several years, and the herculean efforts of William H. Emory, to settle. The boundary report was finally completed in 1857, and the map by Emory which it contained (Plate 44), depicted not merely the narrow limits between the two countries, but showed the entire United States west of the Mississippi with an accuracy and detail previously unknown.

A short time after the Mexican War gold was discovered at Sutter's Mill on the American River in the new U.S. Territory of California, and Texas found itself on the route of many of the gold seekers bound for California. To assist the forty-niners, the Texas Legislature and the United States Army independently authorized surveys to determine the most practical routes across the arid deserts of West Texas. The earliest of these surveys was led by Texas Ranger Capt. John Coffee Hays, who in the fall of 1848 went due west from San Antonio as far as the Pecos. A second survey was undertaken that same year by two other well-known Texas Rangers, John S. Ford and Robert S. Neighbors, who traveled from Austin all the way to Franklin on the Rio Grande, now known as El Paso.

While Ford and Neighbors concentrated on locating what was to be called the Upper California Road, another survey under Capt. W. H. C. Whiting of the Corps of Topographical Engineers explored a more southerly route to El Paso, which would in turn become known as the Lower California Road. Both of these parties returned to San Antonio in the summer of 1849. The routes they pioneered were examined in greater detail the same year by two expeditions by the Corps of Topographical Engineers. Lieutenant Francis T. Bryan mapped the Upper Road, while the commander of the Corps in Texas, Lt. Col. Joseph E. Johnston, examined the Lower Road. Meanwhile, Capt. Randolph B. Marcy had escorted a party of emigrants from Fort Smith, Arkansas, to Santa Fe across the Texas Panhandle. On his return he explored a more southerly route from Emigrants Crossing on the Pecos

northeast to the Red River near present Sherman. This route was soon followed by hundreds of emigrants and eventually became the line of the Texas and Pacific Railway across Texas. Thus within a few short years, and because of the pressing need of seeing that the gold seekers had an adequate route to follow, the whole of West Texas was crisscrossed by a succession of exploring parties and emigrant groups. This development paralleled similar activities throughout the entire West as the country moved in one great rush to reconnoiter the lands wrested from Mexico and to explore the new domain. Under the leadership of the Corps of Topographical Engineers, parties explored the entire American West from Mexico to Canada in an attempt to locate the most practical route for a transcontinental railroad. This tremendous undertaking, which has been called the Great Reconnaissance, was concluded in 1857 with the publication of the twelve volume report of the Pacific Railroad Survey. Included in the report was a "Geographical Memoir" by Lt. Gouveneur Kemble Warren and a large map. Warren's map was based on the reports of all the various surveys and succeeded for the first time in accurately depicting the whole of the Trans-Mississippi West.

At the time of annexation, the frontier line in Texas ran from the Nueces River above San Patricio to just west of San Antonio, then northeast past New Braunfels and Austin, which were then on the extreme western edge of civilization. From there it made a sweeping curve to the east far past present Waco, and then turned back west past Dallas and the settled portions of the Peters Colony. The Army was charged with responsibility of exploring routes across West Texas for the emigrants to travel and with defending this frontier against Indian attacks. In carrying out this task, the Army established in 1849 a line of forts paralleling the frontier, similar to the line of Ranger blockhouses a decade earlier. This line of eight posts from Fort Duncan on the Rio Grande to Fort Worth in the north shielded the frontier settlements. So rapidly did settlers push west, however, that more forts were soon needed, and in the 1850s a new line of seven forts was constructed, curving from Fort Clark on the Rio Grande through Fort Concho in the west to Fort Belknap in the north. During the same period it was necessary also to construct forts Lancaster, Stockton, Davis, and Quitman to protect the routes to El Paso.

Cheap land continued to stimulate settlement on the western and southwestern frontier. It was still free to the settlers in the empressario colonies established as late as 1848, and in 1854 a homestead act awarded 160 acres to settlers on the public domain. Great quantities of land scrip and certificates, redeemable in unlocated land, were in circulation, and surveying crews led by such avid land speculators as Jacob de Cordova braved the Indian menace to locate, establish meets and bounds, and lay claim to western lands. The Texas General Land Office was flooded with surveys as it granted titles to millions of acres.

The rapid increases of the population occasioned by the availability of cheap land indicated the potential for a booming economy, but development was hindered by the tremendous size of the state and the lack of adequate transportation facilities. In 1850 no single stage line or railroad existed, and development and maintenance responsibilities of the roads themselves were delegated to the individual counties. Principal roads linked county seats and major towns, but these were rough and difficult at best, while the lesser roads often ended at the county line. While numerous small stage lines connected major points, the only one of any length was the great Butterfield Overland Mail Company which, beginning in 1857, crossed Texas from Grayson County in the east to El Paso in the west. Freight was likewise carried by numerous independent muleskinners; it was both slow and expensive. River navigation was a significant factor in antebellum Texas, but the shallow channels clogged with sandbars and rafts making even this traditional solution to transportation problems

hazardous. Texas clearly needed a system of adequate railways, but financing construction was such an obstacle that the first track was not laid until 1852. A law in 1854 provided land grants of sixteen sections for each mile of track laid, and this resulted in the chartering of several companies, but by 1861 a total of only 492 miles of track were operating, hopelessly inadequate for the needs of the state. Secession and the Civil War brought an end for a time to any further construction.

The period between the Mexican War and the Civil War brought the most dramatic increases in geographical information about the interior of Texas in its history. Beginning with the early surveys for routes to California, this information was brought to public attention virtually as soon as it was discovered. Almost all of the military surveys, such as those by Johnston and Marcy, resulted in published reports with maps. These, as well as the information from other surveys, were utilized by promotional works such as the map and guidebook published in 1849 by Robert Creuzbaur, *Route from the Gulf of Mexico and the Lower Mississippi Valley to California. . . .* Jacob de Cordova as early as 1848 commissioned Creuzbaur to produce a map of Texas in the interest of promoting his various land schemes (see Frontispiece; Plate 39). Drawn from the records of surveys in the General Land Office, it is perhaps the first large scale map of the state to be based on cadastral surveys.

Similarly the additional colonies and land ventures which were chartered under state law, such as the *Adelsverein's* enterprise near New Braunfels, produced promotional maps and guidebooks to illustrate their tracts (Plate 41). In 1855 de Cordova retained a Land Office draftsman, Charles W. Pressler, to revise his 1849 map, and the next year Pressler decided to produce his own. Published in 1858, Pressler's map (Plate 46) was based on the latest reports in the General Land Office and was the first accurately detailed depiction of the state. The Mexican Boundary Survey produced not only the official report containing Emory's important map, but also a host of other reports, documents, memoirs, and personal narratives. Each of these were illustrated with maps depicting the work of the survey and at times justifying controversial decisions.

All of these original productions were utilized by the commercial ateliers to produce maps for the trade. One of the emerging publishers of importance was J. H. Colton. His 1849 map of California, Oregon, and Texas illustrated the popular preoccu-

pation with the Gold Rush, westward expansion, and Manifest Destiny. It was typical of many such maps produced by other publishers like Mitchell, Wyld, and Young. Colton also produced a lavish and influential wall map of North America in 1849 on which he portrayed all of the recent explorations (see Plate 43). Finally, the maps of the U.S. Coast and Geodetic Survey began to reveal the Texas coast in its true outline for the first time during this period (Plate 42).

END OF THE FRONTIER

Secession and the Civil War halted not only railroad construction but also all exploration and westward movement. At the outset of the war, the frontier line extended northwest from Nueces County to Uvalde west of San Antonio, and then northeast to the Red River. With the outbreak of hostilities, federal troops were either withdrawn from their frontier posts or surrendered, and after the war they were not immediately replaced. During this interim the western frontier of Texas was ravished as never before by Comanche and Kiowa raids. After the war the residents of the frontier expected the U.S. Army to re-establish the string of forts that protected them from the marauding Indians. The Army, though, was stretched thin by its occupation duties, and it was several years before they were able to take such action. During 1867 and 1868 a number of posts were re-occupied and rebuilt. More vigorous military operations against the Indians did not begin until 1871, but a series of expeditions under Ranald S. Mackenzie over the next four years quickly succeeded in blunting the thrusts of the hostile attacks. By the summer of 1875, the Indian barrier to the settlement of the frontier was ended in Texas, and the Comanche and Kiowa bands were confined to reservations in the Indian Territory. With the end of the Indian wars came the end of the active participation of the military in the exploration and mapping of the state.

The Civil War also had caused a major disruption in the cattle trade in South Texas. The large herds there, originating in the Spanish cattle raising enterprises of the colonial period, had fed the markets of Texas and Louisiana before the war. Because transportation of the cattle to market was almost impossible during the war, the herds were not thinned and natural multiplication resulted in a near-geometric increase in their numbers. By the close of the war there were probably ten times as many cattle as people in Texas. At the same time an enormous demand for beef in the slaughterhouses of the North created the age of the great trail drives, and the routes they followed became an attraction on maps of the period.

The first of the great cattle trails was the Chisholm, which ran from central Texas due north across Oklahoma to the railhead at Abilene, Kansas. This trail avoided the timbered lands of eastern Texas and Oklahoma, and more important, skirted the settlements and farms located there. As the frontier moved west, however, the cattlemen wre forced to take increasingly wider detours to avoid the farms. They soon became squeezed between the farmers and the Indians. When the Indians were confined to the reservation in 1875 it opened the possibility of a new trail, called the Western Trail, which ran from San Antonio to the Santa Fe Railroad at Dodge, Kansas. The cattle drives were hampered by the spread of a disease known as Texas fever, and by 1885 Texas cattle were quarantined from almost all the other states to prevent infection of the local livestock. Although a cure for the disease was discovered in 1889, trail driving did not resume. The westward extension of the frontier and the concomitant fencing of the plains and prairies made trailing impossible; the extension of the railroads into West Texas made it unnecessary.

Reconstruction brought little progress to the building of railroads earlier halted by the war. The Texas Constitution of 1869 forbade the granting of land to railroads to finance construction. But in 1873, the resurgent Democrats in the legislature pushed through a constitutional amendment permitting such grants, and the new Constitution of 1876 authorized allotments of sixteen sections of public land per mile of track laid. In the ensuing years over thirty million acres of land were thus granted to railroad companies.

Few if any of the railroad companies profited by these subsidies. The law required the companies to dispose of the land within eight years of its acquisition, and the state undermined land values by pricing the public domain as low as fifty cents per acre to the settlers. In addition, railroad companies were only entitled to vacant lands in West Texas, and they were required to survey the land and submit field notes before receiving title.

Finally, they were allowed to locate and file only on alternate sections of land, the remainder being reserved for the school fund. In this way almost all of West Texas was surveyed at the expense of the railroad companies, and since the cost of surveying, mapping, and patenting were estimated at about fifty cents an acre, the railroad companies rarely profited from their subsidies. Some, indeed, went bankrupt, and others, instead of alienating the land as required by law, established landholding subsidiaries and began to advertise and develop the land in order to sell it to settlers.

More important to the railroads than land grants were the subsidies offered by the communities along the prospered routes. Most towns were desperate to have railroad connections, and they competed eagerly with their neighbors to offer a more attractive package to the railroad for running the line through their town. These packages often included depots, rights-of-way, and terminal facilities provided at the town's expense, and some even included cash subsidies. Those towns that chose not to participate in subsidies were often by-passed, and many then declined rapidly and even died.

The Texas and Pacific Railroad, chartered in 1871, was perhaps the greatest of the early railroad lines in Texas. Second only to the T&P was the Southern Pacific, which acquired over thirty operating lines in Texas and whose Sunset Route from New Orleans to California through South and West Texas became one of the most famous in the country. Other important lines included the Missouri, Kansas and Texas, which became known as the Katy; the Fort Worth and Denver; the International and Great Northern, which eventually became a part of the Missouri Pacific system; and the Santa Fe.

In 1860 Texas, with less than 400 miles of track, ranked twenty-eighth among the states. By 1900 almost ten thousand miles of track were in operation, placing Texas first in the nation. In 1878, the peak construction year, more miles of track were laid in Texas than in the rest of the states combined. The phenomenal development of the railroads in Texas was the primary factor in the state's settlement and development during the last quarter of the nineteenth century, marking the beginning of the industrialization of Texas.

Other factors important to the westward movement of the frontier of Texas after it was opened following the slaughter of the buffalo and the confinement of the Indians on the reservation, included the rapid alienation of the public domain and the development of new techniques for pioneering the semiarid lands of western America. A series of legislative acts from 1874 to 1895 allowed homesteaders to acquire tracts of land for as little as fifty cents an acre. At first this brought a flurry of land speculation, but as the prices from the state remained low and land available, many speculators failed to make profits. They were followed by a wave of ranchers who snapped up the railroad lands and filled in the alternate sections from the state. Finally, ranchers were succeeded by a movement of homesteaders who, utilizing the "Great Plains techniques" of dry-land farming, gradually took over much of the land from the cattlemen, fenced it, and made it bloom.

The creation of functional local governments along the frontier line was an important factor in the settlement of the region and served as perhaps the best indicator of the westward movement in Texas. The maps of the period, particularly those published in the commercial plants of New York and Philadelphia, revealed the uniform push westward, as tier by tier new counties were formed and organized. The line of settlement indicated by county governments moved westward by two tiers of counties in the 1870s and in the next decade it penetrated the Panhandle and the trans-Pecos. Only 24 of Texas's 254 counties remained to be organized at the turn of the century and hence, for practical purposes, the frontier ended with the nineteenth century.

FILLING IN THE BLANKS

Carl Wheat, the great historian of western American cartography, has pointed out that the 1857 publication of G. K. Warren's large map of the western United States in the reports of the Pacific Railroad Surveys marked the completion of mapping the West in its general form. Since then, Wheat noted, the task of cartographers of the American West has been limited to filling in details. What Warren's map did for the West as a whole was accomplished for Texas that same year by Pressler. He succeeded in outlining the main topographical features in their correct proportions and left to others the task of adding details; for the most part these details consisted of economic, political and cultural features, not topography.

After the Civil War, the United States government commissioned a number of expeditions by prominent scientist-explorers, men like Ferdinand Hayden, John Wesley Powell, and Clarence King, to fill in the details on Warren's map. These expeditions led ultimately to the founding of the U.S. Geological Survey, which organized a comprehensive exploration and mapping effort, utilizing sophisticated geodetic techniques. In Texas, the task of filling in the blanks on Pressler's map fell to a number of agencies. The Coast Survey resumed and completed its charting of the Gulf Coast. The General Land Office of Texas continued collecting plats and surveys, many contributed by the railroads, and in 1879 began issuing a series of county plat maps. In 1884 the U.S. Geological Survey began working in Texas, which resulted in the publication of a number of topographic maps before the end of the century. The State Geological Survey under Edwin T. Dumble contributed a number of reports between 1887 and 1894. But for the most part, published maps of Texas were produced as promotional documents by the railroads and land speculators, or commercially for travelers by such firms as Rand, McNally. By the end of the nineteenth century, Texas had long been mapped and explored. There remained, however, much work of a different kind to be accomplished in the twentieth century. An adequate geologic map of the state was not produced by the Bureau of Economic Geology until 1936, and as late as 1935 the Texas Planning Board listed the completion of topographic maps of Texas for the use of industry as one of its highest goals. But by 1900, when the Geological Survey published Robert T. Hill's map of Texas (Plate 50), the major features of the state had been mapped utilizing the modern techniques of geodesy.

The Texas chapter in the complex story of mapping America proved to be part of a pattern as well as an exception in the patchwork settlement of European societies in a new world. The transfer of cultures from one hemisphere to another would have been extraordinary in any age, but amidst a revolution in scientific knowledge, aided by new techniques in recording, disseminating, and manipulating geographical information, the outcome was recorded in exceptional detail on maps created during four centuries.

The lands to become Texas, like other areas of conquest, experienced intrusion first by sea. Treasure-seekers soon followed, after which the churchmen, the military, the political opportunists, and finally land-hungry settlers introduced themselves into the interior. In Texas, however, these layers of newcomers normally differed in national and cultural origin. The frequency of their enterprises repeatedly mirrored the pulse of European and later American politics. Texas's strategic location made it a showcase of cultural conflict reflected and recorded most effectively in the myriad of cartographic productions detailing its history. Each landmark map served as an introduction to the ones to come.

COLOR PLATES

Abraham Ortelius, *Americae Sive Novi Orbis Nova Descriptio,* 1587
See also p. 73, Plate 5.

46

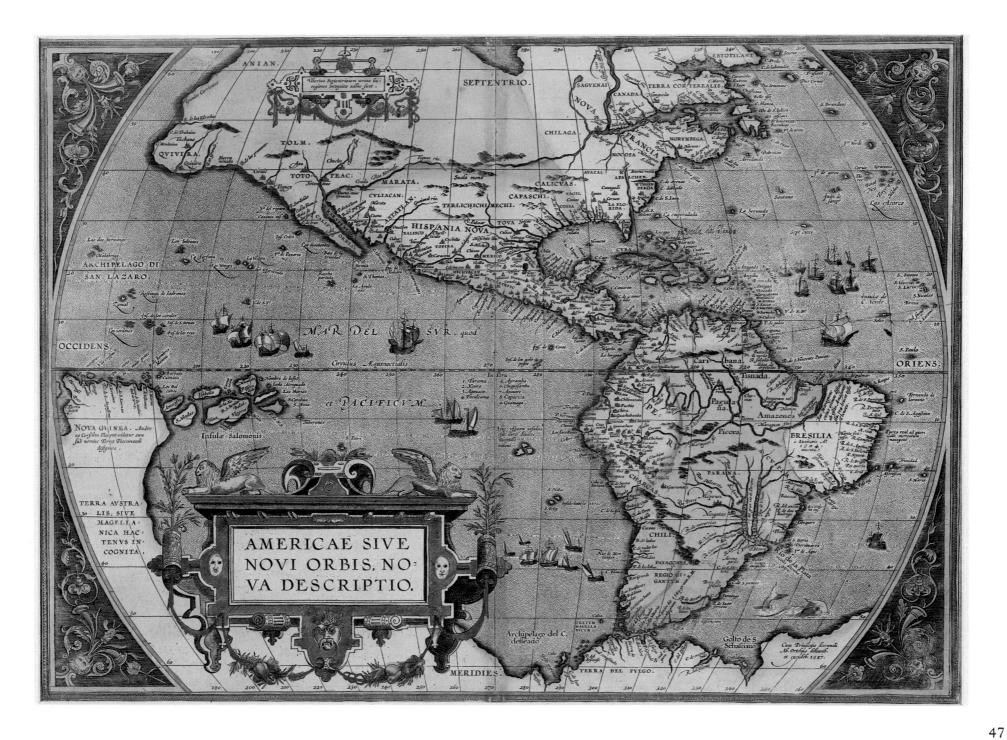

Nicolas de Fer, *Les Costes aux Environs de la Riviere de Misisipi*, 1705
See also p. 91, Plate 13.

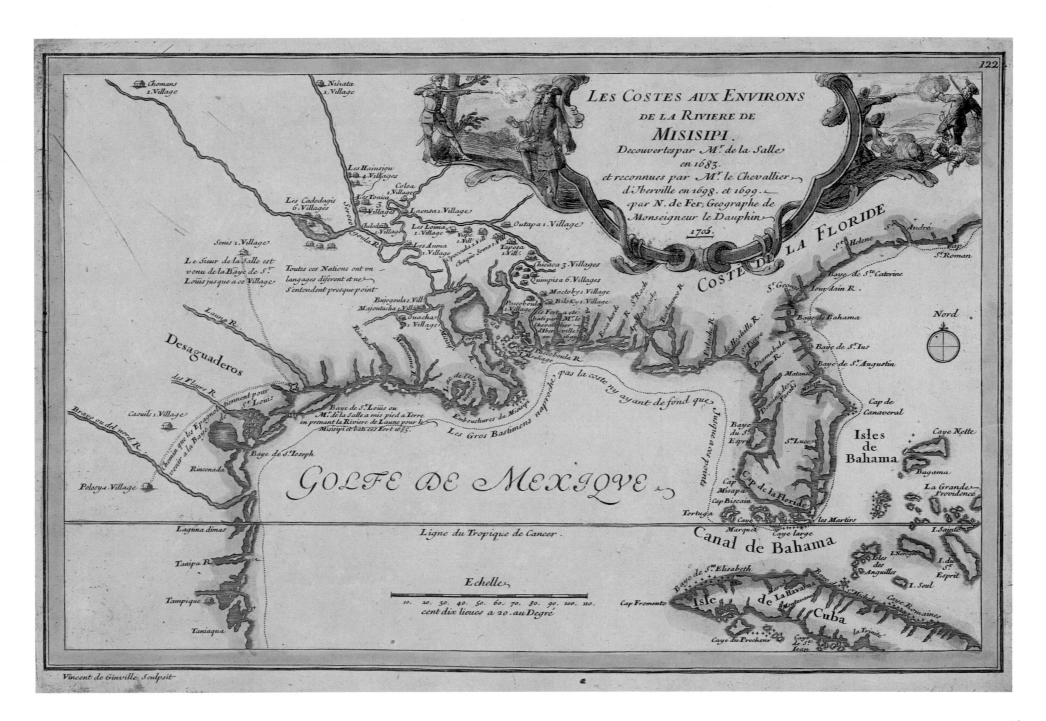

LES COSTES AUX ENVIRONS
DE LA RIVIERE DE
MISISIPI.
Decouvertes par M. de la Salle
en 1683.
et reconnues par M. le Chevallier
d'Iberville en 1698. et 1699.
par N. de Fer, Geographe de
Monseigneur le Dauphin
1705.

Chomans 1.Village

Nihata 1.Village

Les Hainsiou 4.Villages

Coloa 1.Village

Les Cadodagis 6.Villages

Les Tonica 3.Village

Laensa 1.Village

Outapa 1.Village

André

St Roman

Senis 1.Village

Les Loma 1.Village

Les Auma 1.Village

Wape 1.Vill.

Opocoula 1.Vill.

Taposa 1.Vill.

Chaque Soma 1.Vill.

Ste Helene

Baye de Ste Caterine

COSTE DE LA FLORIDE

Le Sieur de la Salle est venu de la Baye de S.t Loüis jusque a ce Village

Toutes ces Nations ont vn langages diferent et ne s'entendent presque point

Chicaca 3.Villages

Quimpis a 6.Villages

Moctoby 1.Village

Bilo Ky 1.Village

Bujogoula 1.Vill.

Majoutacha 1.Vill.

Ouacha 1.Village

Pascoboula 1.Village

Le Fort a été bati par M. le chevallier d'Iberville en 1699

St George

Iourdain R.

Baye de Bahama

Nord

Desaguaderos

Laune R.

Casuils 1.Village

tiennent pour St Louis

Baye de St Loüis ou M. de la Salle a mis pied a Terre en prenant la Riviere de Laune pour le Misisipi et bâti ces Fort 1685.

Embouchures du Misisipi

Les Gros Bastimens naprochent pas la coste ny ayant de fond que

Jusque a ce point

Matanse

Cap de Canaveral

Baye du St Esprit

St Luce

Isles de Bahama

Caye Nette

Chemin que les Espagnols tiennent pour venir a la Baye de

Bravo ou del nord R.

Rinconada

Baye de S.t Ioseph

Cap Misapa

Cap Biscain

Cap de la Floride

Bugama

La Grande Providence

Polosy 1.Village

GOLFE DE MEXIQUE

Tortuga

les Martirs

I. Sainte

Laguna dimas

Ligne du Tropique de Cancer.

Marquet

Caye large

Canal de Bahama

I. Norigue

Isles des Anguilles

I. du St Esprit

Tanipa R.

Echelle

10. 20. 30. 40. 50. 60. 70. 80. 90. 100. 110.

cent dix lieues a 20. au Degré

Baye de Ste Elisabeth

I. Seul

Tampique

Cap Fromento

Isle de La Havalna **Cuba**

Caye Romaines

Taniaqua

Caye du Precheur

Caye de St Iean

la Trinite

Guillaume Delisle, *Carte du Mexique et de la Floride* . . . , 1703
See also p. 93, Plate 14.

Ph. Buache P.G.d.R. d. l.A.R.d.S. Gendre de l'Auteur Avec Privilege du 30 Av. 1745.

51

Stephen F. Austin, *Map of Texas* . . . , 1830
See also p. 121, Plate 29.

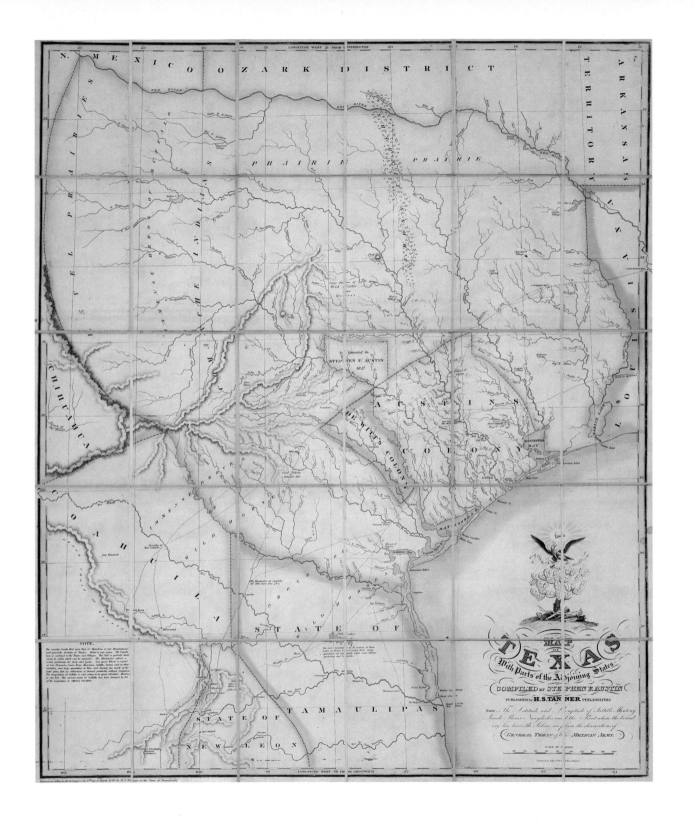

David H. Burr, *Texas*, 1833
See also p. 123, Plate 30.

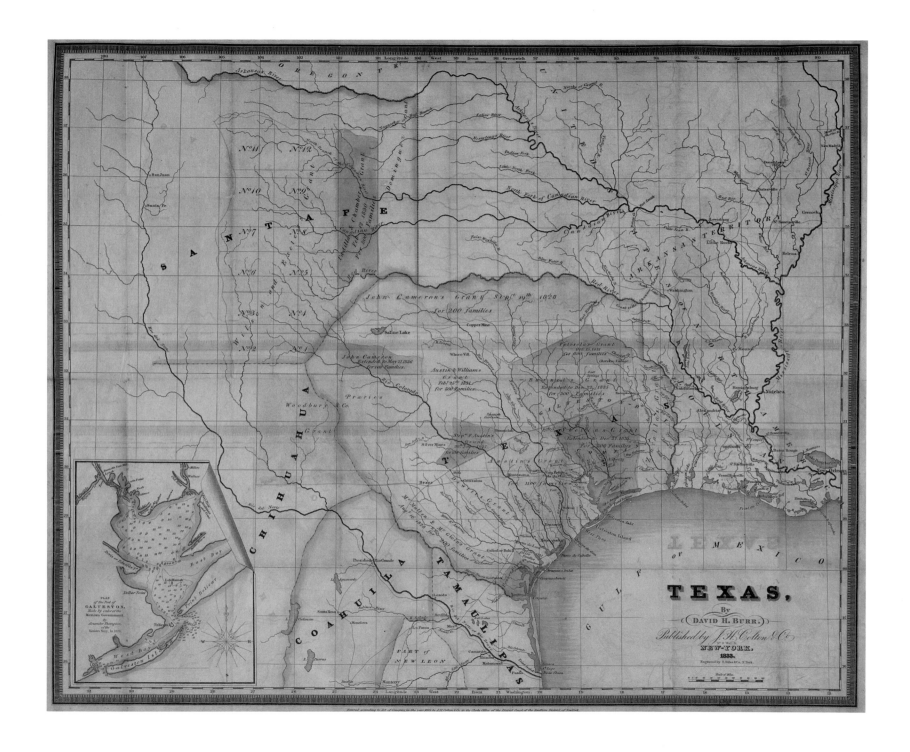

TEXAS,

By
DAVID H. BURR.

Published by J.H. Colton & Co.
NEW-YORK,
1833.

Samuel Augustus Mitchell, *A New Map of Texas, Oregon and California,* 1846
See also p. 135, Plate 36.

57

John Disturnell, *Mapa de los Estados Unidos de Méjico . . .* , 1847
See also p. 137, Plate 38.

59

George Woolworth Colton, *Map of the State of Texas* . . . , 1873
See also p. 159, Plate 48.

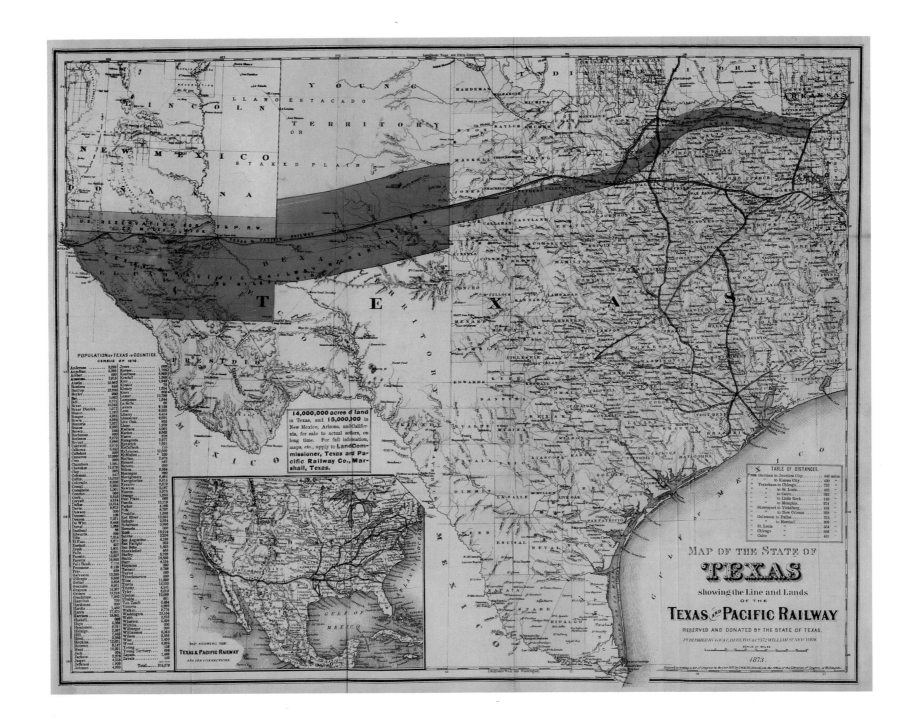

MAP OF THE STATE OF
TEXAS
showing the Line and Lands
OF THE
Texas AND Pacific Railway
RESERVED AND DONATED BY THE STATE OF TEXAS.

PUBLISHED BY G.W.& C.B.COLTON & CO.172 WILLIAM ST. NEW YORK.

1873.

PLATES

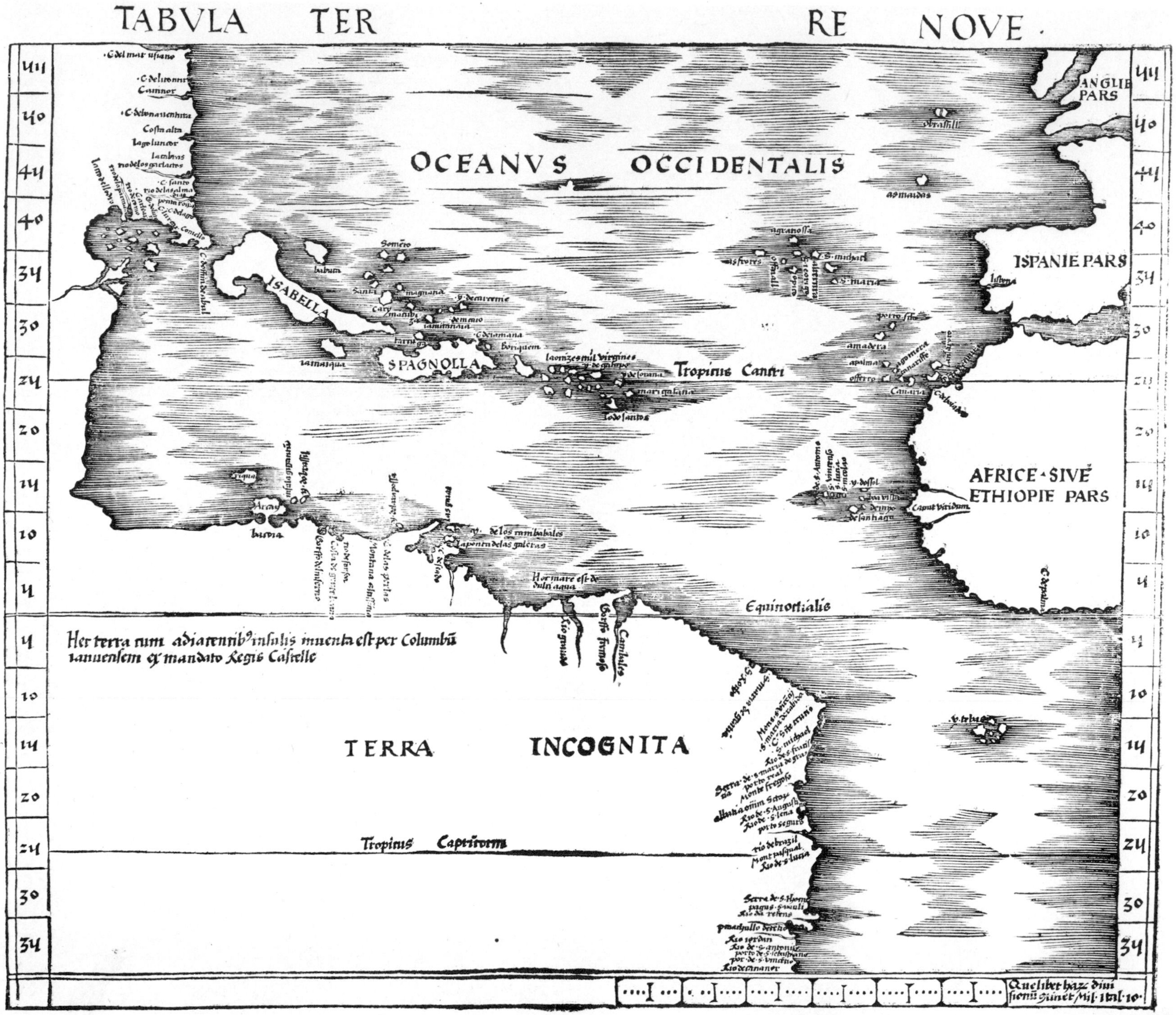

OCEANVS OCCIDENTALIS

ISPANIE PARS

ANGLIE PARS

ISABELLA

SPAGNOLLA

Tropicus Cancri

AFRICE · SIVE
ETHIOPIE PARS

Caput Viridum

Equinoctialis

Her terra cum adiacentib⁹ insulis inuenta est per Columbū
ianuensem ex mandato Regis Castelle

TERRA   INCOGNITA

Tropicus Capricorni

Quelibet haz diui
fionú sunt Mil·leu·10·

64

Plate 1.   Martin Waldseemüller, *Tabula Terre Nove.*

Woodcut; 37 × 44.5 cm (14.5 × 17.5 in.). Published in: Claudius Ptolemy, *Geographie opus novissima Traductione e Grecorum archetypis castigatissime Pressum . . .* (Strasbourg, 1513).

The science of cartography and the art of printing merged in an early and influential partnership in the works of Martin Waldseemüller, a highly accomplished student of geography and a clergyman in the village of St. Dié, approximately 175 miles south of Strasbourg. Living so near a central point of communication and learning for both Germany and northern Italy, he had ready access to the most recent information on world affairs and to scholarly resources as well.

Waldseemüller was born at Radolfszell on Lake Constance between 1470 and 1475. He studied theology at the University of Freiburg and later became Canon at St. Dié, a position he held until his death about 1522. Early in the sixteenth century, he engaged in the study of Ptolemy with a young scholar named Philesius Ringmann and with Walter Ludd, a printer. Together they produced in 1507 the *Cosmographia Introductio,* a study of geography primarily consistent with Ptolemy. To it they added "The Four Voyages of Amerigo Vespucci," only recently issued as *Mundus Novus,* and two maps, "A Reproduction of the Entire World, both in the Solid and Projected on the Plane, Including also Lands which were Unknown to Ptolemy, and Have been Recently Discovered." Ignorant of the voyages of Columbus, Waldseemüller gave Amerigo Vespucci full credit for these discoveries and forever honored him by giving to this land the name *America.* He justified his actions with an explanation in the text:

Inasmuch as both Europe and Asia received their names from women, I see no reason why any one should justly object to calling this part Amerige, i.e., the land of Amerigo, or America, after Amerigo, its discoverer, a man of great ability.

By the time Waldseemüller learned of Columbus, his book had achieved a wide distribution and the leading map makers of the day copied it freely, giving the name "America" a permanent place in history.

Immediately after completing his first book, he began work on a new edition of Ptolemy's *Geography,* which he published at Strasbourg in 1513, marking a permanent departure from the atlases of Ptolemy. He divided the atlas into two parts: the first contained the traditional twenty-seven maps "intact and separate" in their "ancient form," and a second part to include twenty supplement maps offering "a representation of the three parts of the world more proper to our time." For the first time, then, geography was recognized as a changing science.

The twenty-seven Ptolemaic maps in the atlas were drawn on the trapezoid, or Donis, projection except for the world map, drawn on Ptolemy's conic projection. Other than the map of Northern Europe, all of the modern maps, including the *Tabula Terre Nove* were made on the quadratic plane projection. All of these maps were graduated in latitude, but none attempted to show longitude.

The *Tabula Terre Nove* was one of the earliest, influential printed maps to show a delineation of the Gulf of Mexico. From the earlier Canerio map, a peninsula, possibly Yucatan, was shown as an island and the two continents were shown connected. Significantly, the name *America* was omitted and in its place, Waldseemüller inserted the statement that "this land with the adjoining islands was discovered by Columbus the Genoese under the authority of the King of Castile." Because of this recognition and of the possibility that he had documents attributed to Columbus, this map is frequently referred to as the "Admiral's Map."

Below this line he described the lack of knowledge of the interiors with the simple label, "Terra Incognita." The island of "Isabella," present-day Cuba, was greatly oversized in proportion to the Gulf of Mexico, but the map suggested clearly that the lands surrounding the Gulf were known quite early in the process of discovery. The map was not a prototype for subsequent cartographers because it was quickly outdated. But because Waldseemüller's 1507 maps showing the New World were somehow lost to historians for four centuries, this map long represented to scholars the best and earliest state of knowledge of the New World.

References: Lowery 9; Phillips, *Atlases* 359; Kohl 32.

James Perry Bryan Collection, Barker Texas History Center, The University of Texas at Austin.

†For explanation of abbreviations in references see Sources Cited, page 165.

INDIA fuperior

Cathay

Quinfay

Archipelagus 7448 infularũ

Zipangri

Inf. ꝓdonum

Chamaho

Temiftitan

Panuco· Inf. Tortucarũ

Iucatana

Cozumila

S. Paul

Beragua

Catigara

Nouus orbis

Insula Atlantica quam uocant Brafilij & Americam.

Inf. infortunata

Die Nüw Welt

Regio Gigantum

Calenfuan

Mare pacificum

Fretum Magaliani

Terra florida

FRANCISCA

C. Britonum

Corteraa

Exteriores

Oceanus occidentalis

Hifpania

Medera

Fortunatæ inf.

CVBA

Hifpaniola

Seuilla

Iamica

Antille

Inf. Hefperidum

Dominica

S. Iacobi

PARIA S abundat auro & margaritis

Canibali

AFRICAE pars

Sinus Atlanticus

7. infule Margueritarũ

66

Plate 2.   Sebastian Münster, *Tabula Novarum Insularum.*

Woodcut; 25.5 × 34 cm (10 × 13.5 in.). Published in: Sebastian Münster, *Cosmographiae Universalis . . .*
(Basel, 1550).

The German humanist movement of the Renaissance produced many versatile scholars; typical of these was Sebastian Münster. Although he was the foremost German geographer of his day and was hailed by later generations as "the German Strabo," he was better known to his contemporaries for his work in other fields. Born in 1488 in the German Rhineland, Münster was educated at the great Renaissance university at Heidelberg, where he was schooled not only in the classics, Hebrew, and Greek, but also in the mathematical and scientific principles of his age. In 1529 he was appointed to the chair in Hebrew at the University in Basel, and his studies in that field were soon known across Europe. Basel, the oldest Swiss university, was at that time the intellectual center of the German Renaissance and the home of such influential figures as Erasmus of Rotterdam, the foremost humanist, and Hans Holbein, the well-known artist. It was also distinguished as a center for the publication of scholarly books and for wood engraving.

Münster made his first map as early as 1525, and before 1537 had issued several maps and geographical books based on information gleaned from a network of scholars throughout Europe. In 1538 he published critical editions of the descriptive geographies of the ancient writers Pomponius Mela and Caius Julius Solinus, to which he added his own maps. In 1540 Münster was the driving force behind the publication of a new edition of Ptolemy, in which he followed in the footsteps of another influential Rhineland geographer, Martin Waldseemüller, by juxtaposing the ancient Ptolemaic maps with a set of twenty-one new ones (see Plate 1). The Basel edition of the *Geography*, with Münster's maps, was reprinted in 1542, 1545, and 1552.

In 1544 Münster completed his own great work, the *Cosmographia Universalis*, a complete compendium of all the geographical information he had gathered over the decades. It has justifiably been called a true mirror of all that was then known concerning the geography, cartography, and history of the world, its popularity being rivaled only by Ptolemy's *Geography*. It was translated into five languages and reprinted in forty-six separate editions, the last in 1650—over a century after it was first produced.

Münster's map of the New World was first published in his 1538 edition of Solinus; it subsequently appeared in the four editions of Ptolemy and virtually all of the editions of the *Cosmographia*. It was an excellent example of the woodcut process, employing the common technique of supplying the place names by means of metal types inserted into the wood block. These names could be easily interchanged as needed for editions in different languages, and states of the map appeared in Latin, German, French, and other languages.

Münster presented a remarkably advanced outline of the American continents, especially considering that less than fifty years had elapsed since the first voyage of Columbus. He depicted the New World as one land mass and confirmed Waldseemüller's christening of the continents after Vespucci by appending the name "American" in South America. He clearly had firsthand reports of recent explorations at his disposal, and his delineation of North America followed closely the exemplar of Giovanni da Verrazzano after his voyage of 1524. The Italian navigator, when sailing off the coast of what is now the Outer Banks of North Carolina, mistook Pamlico Sound for the Pacific Ocean, a tantalizingly short distance across a narrow neck of land. This so-called Sea of Verrazzano was shown by Münster nearly cutting North America in two, and it in turn opened into a mythical strait connecting the Atlantic with the Pacific. This depiction, along with the place names "Francisca" and "Terra Florida," apportioning the continent between the French and the Spanish, appeared here on a printed map for perhaps the first time and must have contributed substantially to the wide currency of Verrazzano's ideas. Münster also knew definitely of Magellan's discoveries since he appended that explorer's name to the straits south of the mainland. Although Münster presented a good delineation of the Gulf of Mexico, he mistakenly showed Yucatan as an island, and his rendering of Temistitan (Tenoxtitlan, or Mexico City) gave it an erroneous connection with the Gulf. Interior details to the north were nonexistent.

Münster interestingly combined the factual material he had at hand with the folkore and myth he must have derived in part from Solinus. The "Regio Gigantum" (region of the giants) in South America, the archipelago of 7,448 islands near Japan, and the depiction of a cannibal's hut complete with dismembered leg are all examples of this influence.

Münster's map of the New World was probably the single most widely distributed map of America of the age. His rendering of a single land mass, the confirmation of the name America, and the dissemination of the misinformation of Verrazzano combine to make it an important step in the cartographic history of the region.

References: Wheat 20; Lowery 46; Kohl 58; Phillips, *Atlases* 365, 367, 368, 370; *World Encompassed* 272; Wagner, *Northwest Coast* 31; Klemp 9.

Collection of Mr. and Mrs. Jenkins Garrett, Fort Worth, Texas.

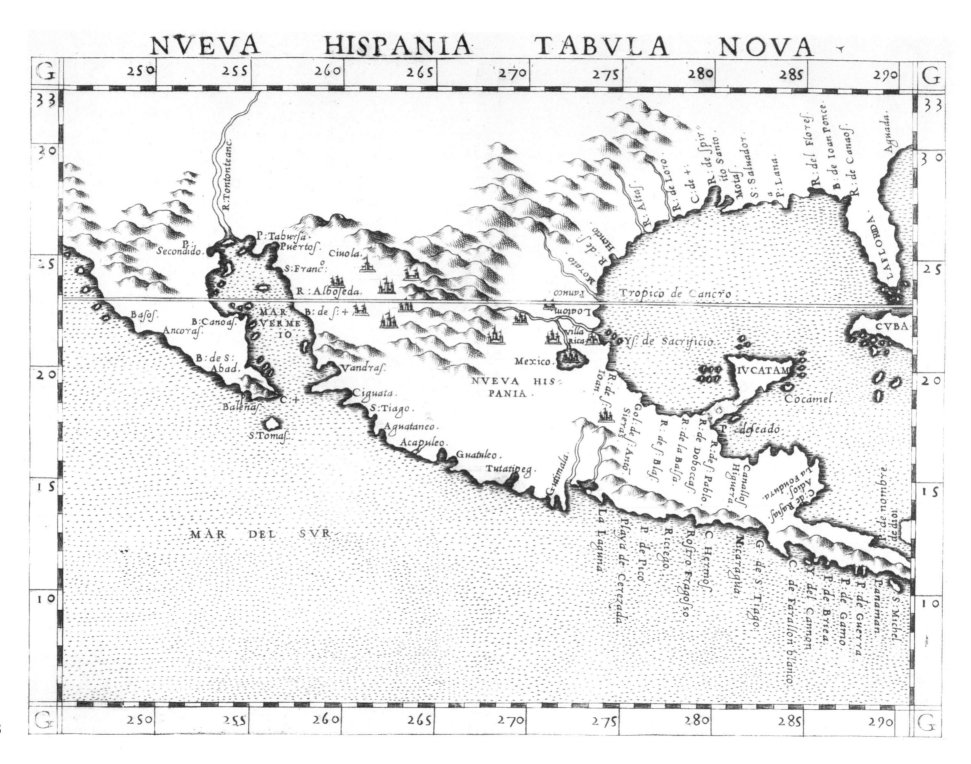

Plate 3. Girolamo Ruscelli, *Nueva Hispania Tabula Nova.*

Engraving; 22.5 × 30.9 cm (8.9 × 12.1 in.). Published in: Claudius Ptolemy, *La Geografia* . . .
(Venice, 1561).

Münster's *Cosmography,* (Plate 2) with its massive text interspersed with woodcut maps and views, vignettes and pictures, was characteristic of the German descriptive geography of its period and thoroughly in the tradition established by the Nuremberg *Chronicle* half a century earlier. To the south in Italy, however, a more graphic tradition prevailed. Here the compilation of manuscript sailing charts, called *portolanos,* had flourished since the fourteenth century. In Italy, too, the craft of engraving on copper, and the business of selling the prints produced by this method, had long been established independent of the bookseller's trade. About 1540 engravers began to include maps in their repertoire of prints; the greater control over line by a cartographer working in copper rather than wood quickly established engraving as the dominant process in the Italian map trade.

In 1548 in Venice the master Italian cartographer Jacopo Gastaldi, working from Sebastian Münster's text and using his maps as a source, produced a new edition of Ptolemy's *Geography.* In this work Gastaldi abandoned the woodcut and engraved the maps on copper, producing the first set of engraved maps since the 1508 edition of Ptolemy. Thereafter not a single edition of the *Geography* was printed with woodcut maps, and the transition to engraving was complete.

Gastaldi also added a complete series of plates of the New World to Ptolemy, including the first map specifically devoted to New Spain.

It was a notable improvement over previous depictions of the area, but committed several egregious errors, such as showing Yucatan as an island.

Thirteen years later another edition of Ptolemy appeared in Venice, based on a new translation from Greek and including extensive addenda by the noted geographer Girolamo Ruscelli. The maps were for the most part simple enlargements of the famous maps by Gastaldi in the previous edition, but there were important innovations. The world map was for the first time divided into two hemispheres, one representing the Old World and one the New. The map of New Spain was significantly improved, correctly showing Yucatan as a peninsula. The place names along the upper Gulf Coast revealed the explorations of Piñeda, Cabeza de Vaca, and Moscosso, and the Mississippi, here shown as the "Rio de Spiritu Santo," was carefully depicted. The map enjoyed wide influence, appearing in successive editions of Ptolemy in 1562, 1564, 1573, 1574, 1596, 1597, and 1599.

References: Nordenskiold p. 26; Phillips, *Atlases* 371, 372; Wagner, *Northwest Coast* 48.

Collection of Mr. and Mrs. Jenkins Garrett, Fort Worth, Texas.

AMERICAE SIVE
NOVI ORBIS, NO-
VA DESCRIPTIO.

Plate 4.   Abraham Ortelius, *Americae Sive Novi Orbis Nova Descriptio.*

Engraving; 36 × 50 cm (14 × 19.6 in.). Published in: Abraham Ortelius, *Theatrum Orbis Terrarum*
(Antwerp, 1570).

Each succeeding decade following the first New World discoveries created its own revolution of knowledge, but a watershed in the growth and compilation of geographical information was the atlas published in 1570 by Abraham Ortelius, a businessman native to Antwerp.

Ortelius was born in 1527, and at an early age his father's death forced him to share financial responsibility for his family. He began working in the coloring of maps, which led him into other businesses requiring extensive travel. He became associated with an influential Dutch entrepreneur, Gilles Hooftman, and early in his career he became friends with Christopher Plantin, a talented printer, and Gerard Mercator, one of the most creative and exacting cartographers of the time.

With the increasing demand for accurate maps from commercial enterprises, Ortelius decided to assemble the best available maps, rework them into a standard size and format, and issue them, with appropriate credit to the authors, as one new atlas. This complete disregard for the Ptolemy-based maps as scientific considerations resulted in his first production, later styled "the first modern atlas," and its immediate and immense popularity created a new perspective for the map trade.

Typical of the magnificent engraving and printing of the Dutch, the atlas's world map and its *Americae Sive Novi Orbis Nova* (America, or new world, newly described) rested largely upon Mercator's great world map of 1569, especially the distorted shape of South America. Place names in the heartlands of North America, also from Mercator, originated with the explorations of Fray Marcos de Niza and of Francisco Vásquez de Coronado. Although greatly exaggerated westward, North America was correctly shown with California as a part of the mainland, and the entire continent was indefinitely divided between New Spain and New France.

Its immediate influence was recognized in 1573 when Ortelius was named Geographer to his Majesty, King Phillip II. The great popularity of the "Theatrum" resulted in many editions printed in Latin, German, French, Dutch, Spanish, English, and Italian from 1570 to 1612, fourteen years after Ortelius's death.

References: Wheat 14; Wagner, *Northwest Coast* 80; *World Encompassed* 135–36; Lowery 56; Nordenskiold p. 124; Kohl 72; Phillips, *Atlases* 374; Koeman Ort 1 (2).

San Jacinto Museum of History, Houston, Texas.

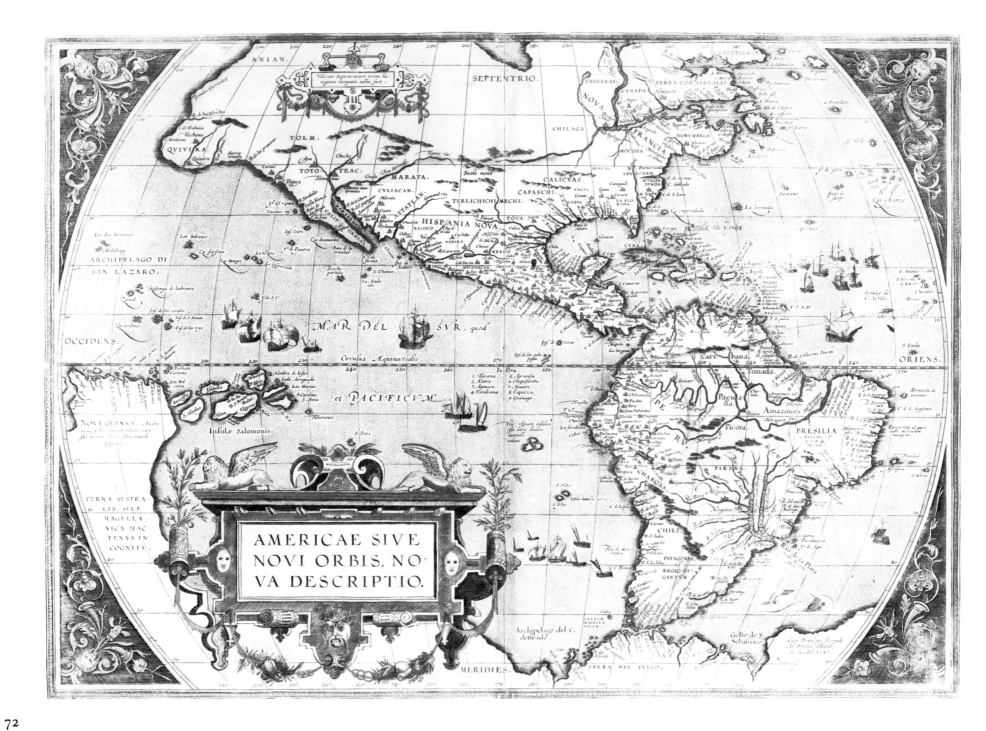

AMERICAE SIVE NOVI ORBIS, NOVA DESCRIPTIO.

72

Plate 5. Abraham Ortelius, *Americae Sive Novi Orbis Nova Descriptio.*

Engraving; 36 × 50 cm (14 × 19.6 in.). Published in: Abraham Ortelius, *Theatrum Orbis Terrarum*
(Antwerp, 1587).

Ortelius, as a compiler and publisher of geographical information, relied heavily upon explorers, travelers, and geographers as sources of primary information. Those map makers whose works he incorporated were listed in a "Catalog of Authors" in most editions of the *Theatrum Orbis Terrarum.* His hard work to keep the atlas current was evidenced by the expansion of this list from 87 names in the original 1570 edition to 127 by the time of Ortelius's death in 1598. The 53 sheets carrying 70 maps in the frist *Theatrum* grew to 119 sheets with over 140 maps in 1598.

Adding new maps, however, was only one way in which the atlas was improved. As was customary with copperplate engravings, a number of plates were reworked over the years, incorporating new materials into the existing map. Skilled craftsmen, such as Frans Hogenberg and his assistants Ambrosius and Ferdinand Arsenius, who engraved virtually all of the plates for Ortelius's *Theatrum,* easily amended the engraved image by carefully hammering out the portion of the plate to be reworked, burnishing it smooth, and then re-engraving the changed form.

The map of America was an excellent example of this revision process. In the first edition of 1570 (Plate 4) Ortelius had relied primarily on his friend Gerard Mercator for his depiction of the New World, and he included Mercator's characteristic bulge in the west coast of South America in his map. In the next few decades new information from explorers like Sir Francis Drake forced Ortelius to abandon Mercator's model, and the 1587 edition of the *Theatrum* included a revised map of the Americas, produced from the original plate, incorporating this and other changes. It is significant that the only noticeable change in North America in the revised map is the addition of an ornate cartouche surrounding the Latin words meaning "this territory is as yet unknown."

References: Koeman Ort 22 (5); see also references for Plate 4.

Sid Richardson Collection, Cartographic History Library, The University of Texas at Arlington.

Also as Color Plate I, p. 47.

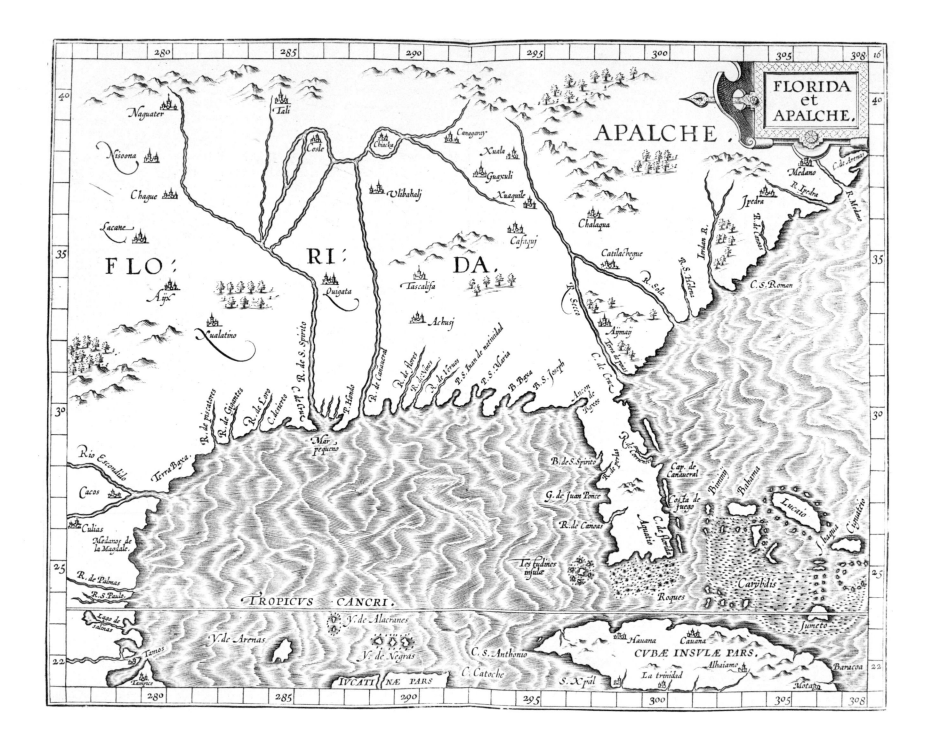

FLORIDA et APALCHE.

APALCHE

FLO RI DA

Naguater
Tali
Cosle
Chiacka
Canagaray
Xuala
Nisoona
Guaxuli
Ulibahalj
Xuaquile
Chague
Chalaqua
Lacane
Casaquj
Catilachegue
Ayx
Quigata
Tascalifa
R. Sola
Xualatino
Achusj
Aymay
R. Secco
Terra de miel
R. de piscatores
R. de Gigantes
R. de Loro
C. desierto
R. de S. Spirito
C. de Cruz
P. Hondo
R. de Cañaueral
R. de Flores
R. Nicbiner
R. de Cruces
P. S. Juan de natiuidal
P. S. Maria
B. Baya
R. S. Joseph
Anton de Bexos
C. de Cruz
R. de perlas
R. de Corentes
Mar pequeño
B. de S. Spirito
Cap. de Cañaueral
Pimini
Bahama

Rio Escondido
Terra Baxa
Cacos
G. de Juan Ponce
Costa de fuego
Lucaio
Culias
R. de Canoas
C. de Aguita
Medanos de la Magdale.
Aquati
Roques
R. de Palmas
Testudines insulæ
R. S. Paulo
Caribdis

Medano
C. de Arenas
Ipedra
R. Ipedra
R. Medano
Jordan R.
R. de Canoas
R. S. Helena
C. S. Roman

TROPICVS CANCRI.

Lago de salinas
Y. de Alacranes
Jumeto
Y. de Arenas
Hauana
Cauana
Tamos
Y. de Negras
C. S. Anthonio
CVBÆ INSVLÆ PARS.
Baracoa
Tampice
C. Catoche
S. Xpal
La trinidad
Alhaiamo
Matan
IVCATINÆ PARS.

74

Plate 6.   Cornelius Wytfliet, *Florida et Apalche.*

Engraving; 23 × 29 cm (9 × 11.4 in.). Published in: Cornelius Wytfliet, *Descriptiones Ptolemaicae Augmentum* (Louvain, 1597); also in: Wytfliet, *Histoire Universelle des Indes* (Douay, 1611).

Cornelius Wytfliet was born in Louvain in the middle of the sixteenth century. Biographical details on him are scarce, but it is known that he was an attorney who rose to the position of secretary to the Council of Brabant, of which Louvain was then capital. He was, in short, a public servant with an interest in geography.

The only known geographic work by Wytfliet, *Descriptiones Ptolemaicae Augmentum,* was published in Louvain in 1597. Although Ptolemy's name was featured prominently in the title, the work itself contained not a word of his *Geography.* Wytfliet announced his purpose in an address to the reader: to supplement the ancient geography of Ptolemy by describing the parts of the world unknown to the Alexandrian geographer. In spite of this avowed worldwide ambition, the *Augmentum* is restricted to America, ignoring the discoveries in Africa and in the East, and can thus be described as the first separately published atlas devoted solely to the Americas.

Wytfliet's work contributed nothing new to the geographical knowledge of the New World. He based his text on the many published accounts of explorations available in the Netherlands in the last decade of the sixteenth century, and his maps reflected this eclectic array of sources. As a compiler instead of a creator, his production has remained all the more valuable as an excellent summary of everything then known in the Spanish Netherlands concerning the New World.

Wytfliet's map of the lands north of the Gulf of Mexico, entitled "Florida et Apalche," plainly was plagiarized from "La Florida" published by Ortelius in the *Theatrum* of 1584, which had been designed for Ortelius by the Spanish geographer Gerónimo Chaves. Chaves was a pilot and noted scientist, and successor to Sebastian Cabot in the Chair of Cartography in the Casa de Contratación, the Spanish clearing-house for new information concerning the Indies. He was also Cosmographer to Philip II, who at the time ruled not only Spain but the Netherlands as well. Privy to all of the official reports of the Spanish explorers, Chaves's map recorded the discoveries of Cabeza de Vaca, de Soto, and Moscoso, and it resembled the manuscript map of a previous Royal Cosmographer, Alonso de Santa Cruz, preserved in the Archives of the Indies. The map revealed little information on the interior of North America, but the details presented have been definitely linked with known features. The village of "Aijx" undoubtedly became known to the Spaniards as Ais, and the Mississippi, though distorted, appeared as the "R. de S. Spiritu," the name given it by early Spanish explorers. The Chaves map published by Ortelius was, therefore, one of the earliest printed maps of the territory based on actual observations, and its reproduction in Wytfliet's popular work helped to correct the previous imaginary concepts of the area.

Wytfliet's *Augmentum* was reprinted in Louvain in 1598; in 1603 it was reissued in Douay, and in 1605 a French translation appeared under the title *Histoire Universelle des Indes.* The work was reprinted three more times, the last one appearing in Arnhem in 1615. The maps in Wytfliet's *Augmentum* have been said to play the same part in the history of cartography of the New World as Ptolemy's maps do for the Old, and they give us a valuable summary of the early cartography of America.

References: Lowery 83; Kohl 264; Wheat 29; Nordenskiold pp. 29, 133; Phillips, *Atlases* 1140, 3644; Koeman Wyt 1 (16); *World Encompassed* 204.

Sid Richardson Collection, Cartographic History Library, The University of Texas at Arlington.

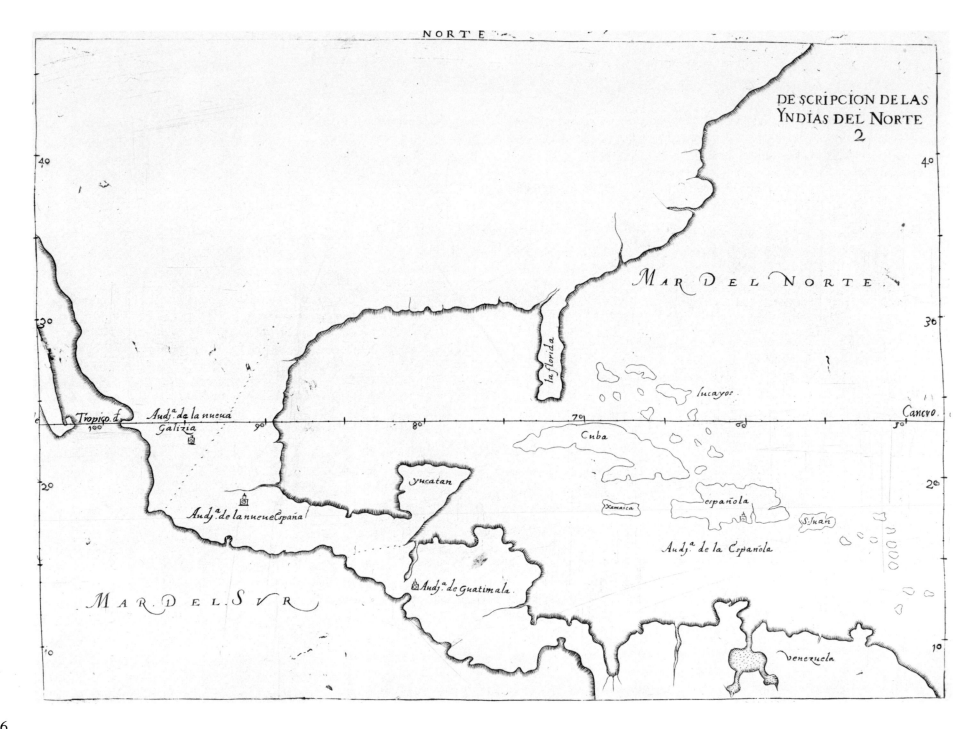

DE SCRIPCION DE LAS
YNDIAS DEL NORTE
2

MAR DEL NORTE

la florida

lucayos

Tropico. d.   Audj.ª de la nueua
Galizia

Cancro.

Cuba

Yucatan

Audj.ª de la nueue España

Xamaica   española   S. Juan

Audj.ª de la Española

Audj.ª de Guatimala

MAR DEL SVR

venezuela

76

Plate 7. Antonio de Herrera y Tordesillas, *Descripción de las Yndias del Norte.*

Engraving; 21.5×28 cm (8.5×11 in.). Published in: Antonio de Herrera y Tordesillas, *Descripción de las Indias Occidentalis* (Madrid, 1601).

Of the colonizing powers in the New World, Spain contributed the least to the growing body of geographical knowledge throughout the centuries of the Great Discoveries. Protective of her gigantic New World empire, Spain kept secret, with few exceptions, as much information as possible, with most of her maps and charts remaining unpublished. Usually only when her ships would suffer piracy from those of the other European powers, and Spanish maps and charts were recovered, did Spain contribute new knowledge to the cartography of the New World.

Yet Spain did permit some compilation and distribution of information concerning the New World, with best work done by Antonio de Herrera y Tordesillas, a well-educated and capable scholar who had rare access to the archives in Spain. Herrera was born in 1559, and after completing his education in Spain, he moved to Italy where he became secretary to Vespasiano de Gonzaga, Viceroy of Naples. Herrera's work for the viceroy led to his appointment by Phillip II as historiographer of Castile and the Indies. Using great care and discretion, Herrera worked through the voluminous archives that documented the early decades of Spanish discovery and exploration. In 1601 he published in four volumes his monumental *Historia general de los hecos de los Castellanos en las Yslas y Tierra Firme del mar Oceano,* which recorded Spain's New World activities from the time of Columbus through 1555. The volumes contained fourteen engraved maps of the West Indies and the countries of Central and South America. The dearth of information on these maps reflects not only the official Spanish position concerning the information it wished disseminated, but also Spanish priorities in exploration and the consequent lack of interior investigations. Interestingly, for the period in which the maps were drawn, the general outlines were essentially correct. California was correctly attached to the mainland and Florida was a peninsula instead of a cluster of islands as it was later shown on some maps. The first edition of Herrera's work, in Spanish, was translated into French and published in Amsterdam in 1622, making the otherwise limited edition more available throughout Europe. Although adding little to the composite knowledge of the Gulf region, Herrera's maps remain as documentation for the claims and attitudes of one of the great New World powers.

References: Lowery 105; Wagner, *Spanish Southwest* 12; *World Encompassed* 231; *Mapas Españoles* 53; Phillips, *Atlases* 1141.

Jenkins Garrett Library, The University of Texas at Arlington.

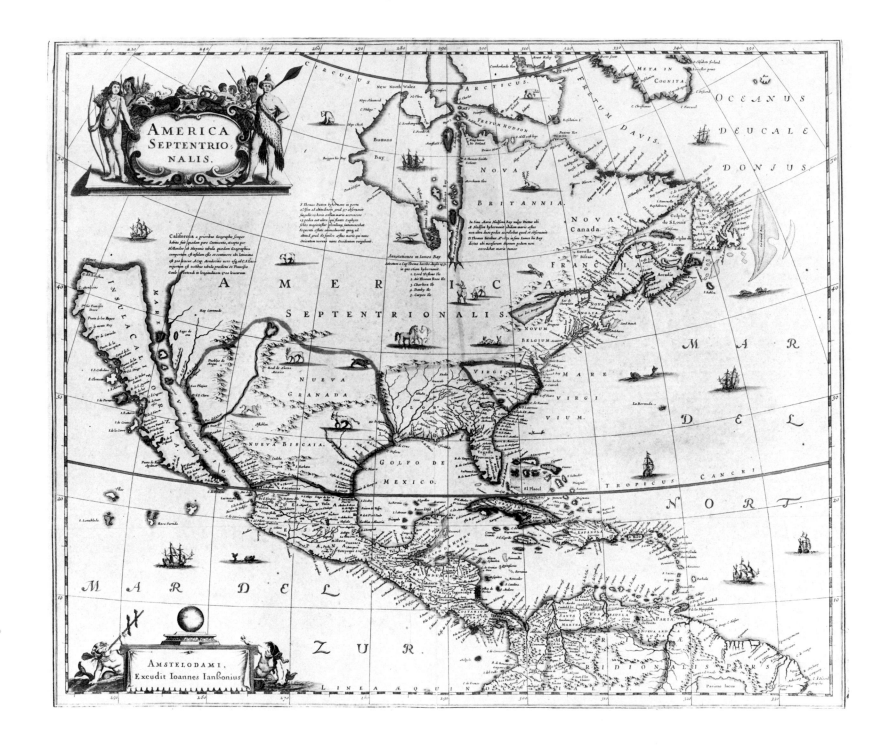

AMERICA
SEPTENTRIO
NALIS.

AMSTELODAMI,
Excudit Ioannes Ianßonius

Plate 8.   Jan Jansson, *America Septentrionalis.*

Engraving; 46.7 × 55.2 cm (18.4 × 21.7 in.). Published in: Jan Jansson, *Novi Atlantis . . .*
(Amsterdam, 1641).

In 1604 Jodocus Hondius, an Amsterdam map and instrument maker who had established a reputation for his magnificent wall maps, purchased the plates to Gerard Mercator's *Atlas* and the Ptolemy from his estate. Within two years he had issued new editions of both of the great master's works and continued to publish updated and expanded versions of the *Atlas* for a number of years. When Hondius died in 1612 his flourishing publishing house was inherited jointly by his sons Jodocus II and Henricus, and by his son-in-law, Jan Jansson. These three continued to issue editions of the *Atlas*, and in 1635 began planning for a totally new work. In 1638 Jansson assumed sole control of the firm and issued his *Atlas Novus*, which, while based on the concept of the great Mercator, was executed according to Jansson's own ideas. The new work enjoyed a reputation almost equal to that of Mercator's, and continued to be published after Jansson's death in 1664.

The two great works of the Mercator-Hondius-Jansson succession, the *Atlas* and *Atlas Novus*, were not completely distinct productions, as many plates used in the former were also incorporated into the latter. The map of North America, for example, was first published in the 1636 Latin edition of the Mercator *Atlas*, and it was not until the 1641 edition of the *Atlas Novus* that Jansson added his own name to the plate. The map represented the popular conception of the continent in the mid-seventeenth century, with a good general outline but lacking in internal details. Although great progress had been made in mapping the Northeast where the explorations of Henry Hudson and Samuel de Champlain had been carefully set down, the lack of information in the Southwest reflected the ignorance of the Spanish concerning their territories and their reluctance in conveying what knowledge they did have to the world at large.

The Mississippi, which had not yet been fully explored, was shown as a vague network of small rivers emptying into the "Baya de la Sp. Santo," located far to the west of the river's actual mouth. The place names along the Texas coast were the same shown by Ortelius over fifty years earlier, while the lack of any interior detail was obscured by a fanciful rendering of a buffalo. The "Real de Nueva España," representing the site of Santa Fe, was carefully placed near the upper course of the Rio del Norte, but that river, confused with the Colorado of the west, was shown emptying into what should be the Gulf of California. California itself was depicted as an island off the coast of the continent rather than as a peninsula. This was a popular misconception which adorned maps of North America for more than a century beginning in 1622, and the legend in the northwest portion of the Jansson map related the origin of this aberration in a Spanish map captured by the Dutch. This legend, along with the ornate title cartouche, covered the complete absence of any depiction of the northwest coast.

Jansson was an extremely influential publisher and this depiction of the continent indicated the best that was known, as well as the great amount that remained unknown, in the period prior to the great French cartographer, Nicolas Sanson.

References: Lowery 128; Wagner, *Northwest Coast* 339; Wheat 45; Koeman Me 122 (486J); *World Encompassed* 142; Phillips, *Atlases* 452, 459, 475, 3422, 4258; Phillips, *Maps* p. 560.

San Jacinto Museum of History, Houston, Texas.

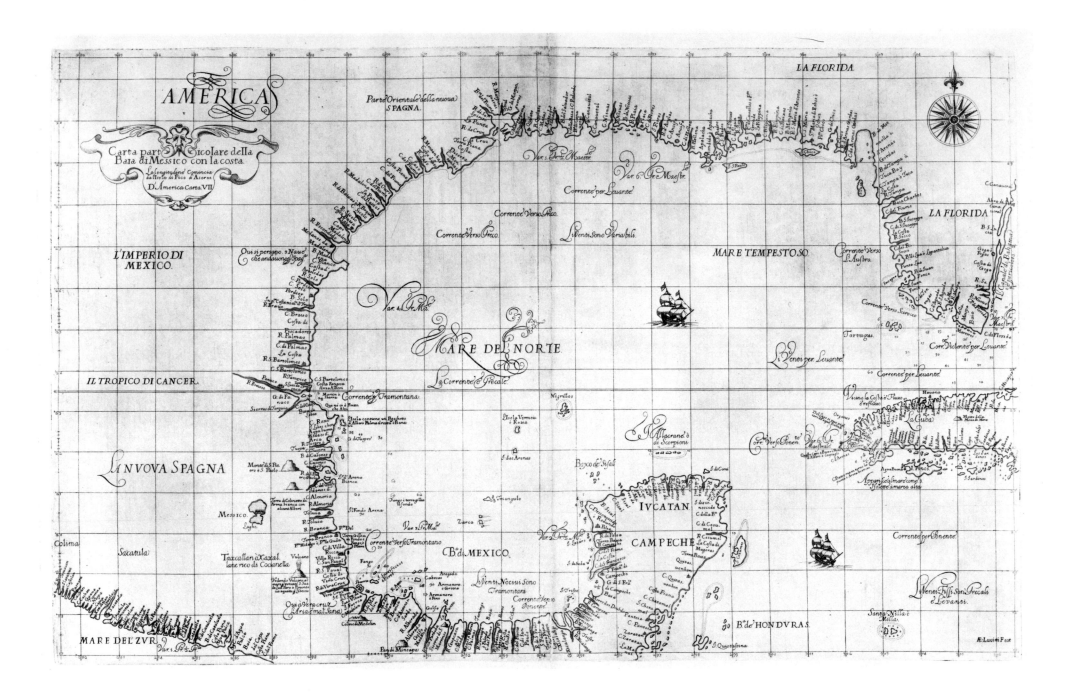

Plate 9.   Robert Dudley, *Carta Particolare della Baia di Messico con la Costa. . . .*

Engraving; 48×75 cm (18.9×29.5 in.). Published in: Robert Dudley, *Dell' Arcano del Mare . . .*
(Florence, 1646–47).

One of the most significant landmarks in the history of cartography, *Dell' Arcano del Mare* ("The Secrets of the Sea"), was produced by an expatriated Englishman living in Florence, Sir Robert Dudley (1573–1649). The three-volume atlas, published in 1646–47, was the first in which all of the maps were drawn on the Mercator projection. In all, it contained 131 maps and charts, as well as mathematical and astronomical tables and information on naval architecture and navigation.

The son of the Earl of Leicester and brother-in-law of the famous Henry Cavendish, Dudley styled himself the Duke of Northumberland and the Earl of Warwick. He was well traveled and well educated and spent much of his adult life working in the preparation of his monumental work. He personally commanded an expedition to the West Indies in 1594–95. His sources for the atlas, predominantly English, were based upon much original, unpublished material, making it a prototype set used by other map makers for many years. His numerous sources for the maps of New England and the East Coast made them among the more extensive in the atlas, but his depiction of the Gulf of Mexico was the first published sea chart of that area and, therefore, had significant influence on later attempts.

The map itself is a beautiful example of the fine copper engraving characteristic of seventeenth century Italy. The map's legends described the currents in the Gulf, and along the coastline numerous rivers were depicted, but their names have little correlation to present-day nomenclature. Typical of the confusion during this period concerning the Texas coastline, Dudley incorrectly placed the "Bay of Espíritu Santo" on the 95th meridian, the site of present-day Galveston Bay.

Although produced when Spain showed little interest in the area we now know as Texas, Dudley's chart of the Gulf of Mexico remained an important source of information for the Texas coastline for many years and quite likely heightened interest for more accurate information in the years that followed.

References: Bryan and Hanak 5; *World Encompassed* 190; Lowery 108; Phillips, *Atlases* 457.

Sid Richardson Collection, Cartographic History Library, The University of Texas at Arlington.

Plate 10. Nicolas Sanson d'Abbeville, *Le Nouveau Mexique et La Floride* . . . (Paris, 1656).

Engraving; 31.5 × 54.7 cm (12.4 × 21.5 in.). Published in: Nicholas Sanson d'Abbeville, *Cartes Generales de Toutes les Parties du Monde* (Paris, 1658).

In the seventeenth century, the demand for knowledge of geographical details of the North American hinterland coincided with the founding of a new school of cartography in Paris by Nicolas Sanson d'Abbeville. Born in 1600, Sanson exhibited in his earliest years special aptitude and interest in the cartographical sciences. His skills established him as a world leader in map production and earned him the title of Royal Geographer to King Louis XIII by the time he was forty years old. He and his followers rejected the Dutch tendencies in the use of heavy ornamentation in the drawing of maps; they emphasized only verifiable information, and as a result their maps accurately record what was known about exploration and discovery. This French school of cartography dominated the map trade for over one hundred years.

As a follow-up to his landmark 1650 cartographic production of North America, Sanson's 1656 *Map of New Mexico and Florida* was the first significant map in a printed atlas to specialize in what is now the American Southwest. For many years it served as a prototype for the delineation of California as an island, and contributed a number of new place names in the New Mexico region, a vast area ranging from the Pacific Ocean on the west to the Florida territory on the east and Canada on the north. It has served as a summary of the best information available for the greater Texas region during the middle of the seventeenth century.

With his 1650 *Map of North America*, Sanson had introduced a great deal of information concerning the nomenclature of American Indians, with words such as "Apache" and "Navajo" appearing on printed maps for the first time. He was also the first cartographer to show Santa Fe as the capital of New Mexico, and in his 1656 map he added the location of a number of new Indian tribes in the New Mexico region. He also continued several traditional errors, such as the placement of "Cibola" and "Quivira," and he contributed some new ones, such as showing the "R. del Norte" flowing into the Gulf of California. Moreover, his prestige and credibility contributed to the longetivity of the error of depicting California as an island.

As a composite of the best information available in Europe concerning this region, the map presented a stark depiction of how little was known about the Texas region prior to the Spanish missionary period. Sanson located a few of the Indian tribes in the Texas region, but the river system clearly was unknown and undescribed—including the great Mississippi.

In spite of its shortcomings, however, the map has continued to be studied as an extraordinary document of the cultural and geographical resources known in the centers of learning in Europe, and it served as an important beginning in the great strides made by French scientists in the eighteenth century.

References: Wheat 50; Lowery 147; Wagner, *Northwest Coast* 374; Tooley, *California* 14; Day 1444.

Collection of Paul C. Ragsdale, New Braunfels, Texas.

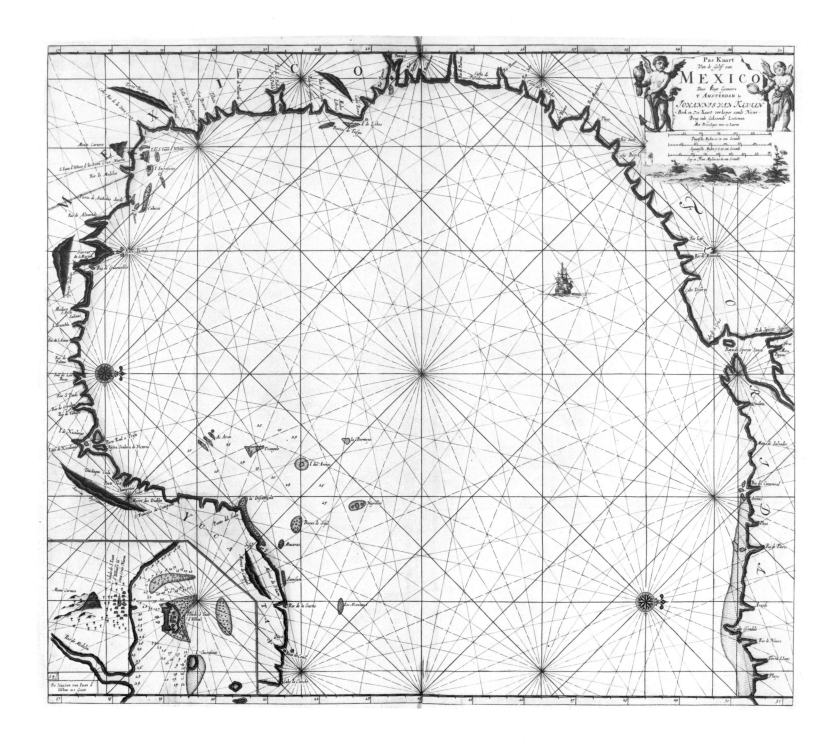

84

Plate 11.   Claes Jansz. Vooght, *Pas Kaart van den Golff van Mexico.*

Engraving: 51 × 58 cm (20 × 22.8 in.). Published in: Johannes van Keulen, *De Nieuwe Groote Lichtende Zee-Fakkel . . .* (Amsterdam, 1684).

The Dutch commercial empire reached its height of power and size during the seventeenth century. The Dutch East India Company, chartered in 1602, replaced the Portuguese in the Far East and assumed a virtual monopoly on trade with India and the Spice Islands. Dutch navigators discovered and named Cape Horn at the tip of South America, and this passage soon replaced Magellan's Strait as the favored passage to the Orient. The Hollanders followed up the explorations of Henry Hudson with the establishment of the first settlement on Manhattan Island, and in 1612 chartered the Dutch West India Company to exploit the loosely-held riches of Spain and Portugal in America. They established colonies in the Caribbean at Caracas, Curaçao, Guiana, and in 1652 wrested the Cape of Good Hope from the Portuguese in South Africa. The Bank of Amsterdam, founded in 1609, succeeded in establishing a sound European coinage, and Amsterdam remained the financial capital of Europe until the French Revolution. One of the major foundations of Dutch power and wealth was their ownership of most of the shipping in northern Europe. Consequently, they were commercial carriers of merchandise, not only between Spain, France, England, and the Baltic, but from the overseas possessions as well.

This enormous traffic in shipping relied heavily on accurate navigational information found in charts and pilot books. These had their origins in small manuscript guides, called "rutters," which served as an aid to the memory of the pilot. As navigation became more scientific and sophisticated, these guides in turn developed into more detailed books and charts intended to light the mariner's way in unknown, or "dark" waters, hence their names "Sea Torch," "Sea Mirror," and "Light of Navigation." The first of these was published in 1584 by Lucas Janszoon Waghenaer. It was so successful that *Waggoner* became the generic term for a sea atlas, and the organization it laid down was followed by almost all later productions. The publication of hydrographic knowledge throughout the seventeenth century was a predominantly Dutch affair, and Waghenaer's book was the model followed by most of the major Dutch publishing houses, including Anthonie Jacobz (known as Lootsman), Jan Jansson, Pieter Goos, Hendrik Doncker, and Willem Janszoon Blaeu. European seamen were dependent on this output of the Amsterdam publishers for their charts and pilot books, and most of these atlases were issued in the major European languages.

The culmination in the development of Dutch pilot books was reached with the publication of *De Nieuvwe Groote Lichtende Zee-Fakkel* by Johannes van Keulen in 1681. Van Keulen, a bookseller specializing in the nautical trade, retained the well-known geographer and mathematician Claes Jansz. Vooght, who compiled the charts for his publication, which was issued serially in five parts, the last in 1683. The work was immediately recognized as superior to anything else on the market and enjoyed a considerable reputation for accuracy and detail. The *Pas Kaart Van de Golff van Mexico* which Vooght constructed for the work appeared in the fourth part, which contained all of the American charts. Oriented with west, rather than north, at the top, common in Dutch sea charts, it represented the most sophisticated rendering of the coast then available. Since its exclusive concern was with navigation, it included no details of the interior.

Johannes van Keulen's son, Gerard, unlike the father, was schooled in mathematics and chart making and compiled many charts himself. He inherited the firm when his father retired in 1704, and he laid its scientific foundation and gave it new impetus. He was named Hydrographer to the Dutch East India Company in 1714. After Gerard's death his sons in turn inherited the firm, and in this way it passed from generation to generation, remaining a viable and important concern, until 1885.

It is no exaggeration to say that the house of Van Keulen, active without break from 1678 to 1885, was the largest nongovernmental hydrographic office in the world. By the second half of the eighteenth century, the advent of scientifically superior sea charts produced by the official hydrographic offices of the European powers, combined with the declining importance of Dutch shipping and commercial centers, diminished the importance of the Van Keulen firm. Nevertheless, the house of Van Keulen was the most important purveyor of hydrographic information in the world for over a century.

References: Phillips, *Atlases* 3444, 3453; Koeman IV:384, (129); Koeman, *Sea on Paper* 44, (14); Lowery 236.

Sid Richardson Collection, Cartographic History Library, The University of Texas at Arlington.

Plate 12. Vincenzo Maria Coronelli, *America Settentrionale* (Venice, 1688).

Engraving; 2 sheets each 60.5 × 45.2 cm (23.8 × 17.7 in.).

Although French scientists dominated the cartographic sciences in the second half of the seventeenth century, other map makers also made significant and lasting contributions. Vincenzo Maria Coronelli, a Franciscan monk who lived most of his life in Venice, added memorable contributions to cartographical sciences, primarily through his production of the largest globes made to date. Perhaps largely through his religious connections, Coronelli had access to geographical information from the explorers then moving throughout the southwestern regions of North America. In 1688 Coronelli issued his *America Settentrionale* . . . , combining the various contributions of knowledge up to that date. His beautiful cartographic productions represented the state of the art of printing. As Royal Geographer to the Republic of Venice, his maps were favorably received by the highest political and scientific circles in Paris and London.

Although he corrected the Sanson mistake of drawing the Rio Grande ("Rio del Norte") as emptying into the Sea of California rather than the Gulf of Mexico (see Plate 10), Coronelli greatly confused the location of the Mississippi River, drawing it in the middle of present-day Texas. Presumably based upon the data of Minet, chronicler of the La Salle expedition, the error might well explain the confusion in La Salle's effort to colonize at the mouth of the Mississippi River.

Coronelli's career spanned the period of French domination in the cartographic sciences: he was born in 1650, the year of the great Sanson map of North America, and he died in 1718, the year Delisle published his landmark map of Louisiana (Plate 19). Although continuing serious errors such as depicting California as an island and his incorrect drawing of the Mississippi River, Coronelli's career marked a step forward through the slow but steady recording of the explorations that brought Texas into the limelight of European politics.

References: Wheat 70; Tooley, *California* 49, 50; Wagner, *Northwest Coast* 434; *World Encompassed* 195.

Sid Richardson Collection, Cartographic History Library, The University of Texas at Arlington.

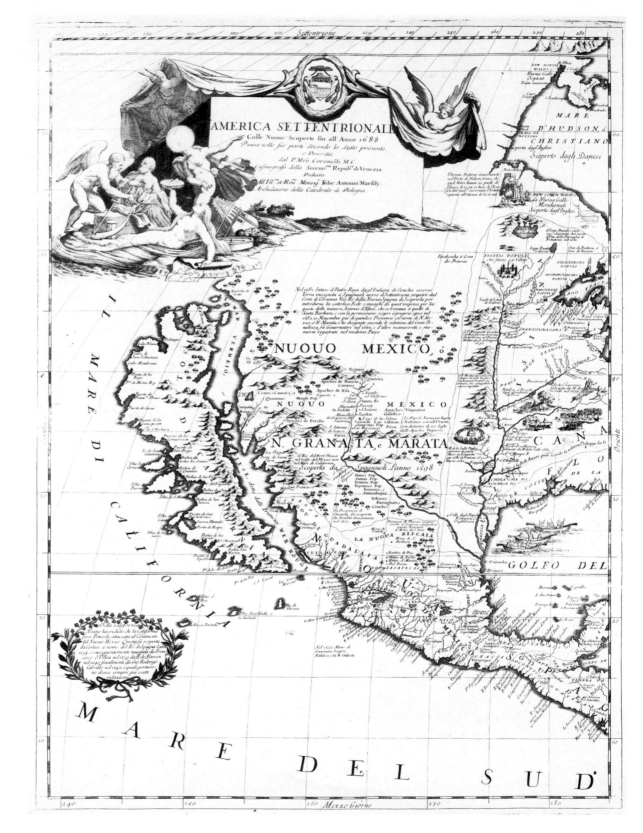

88   Plate 12.

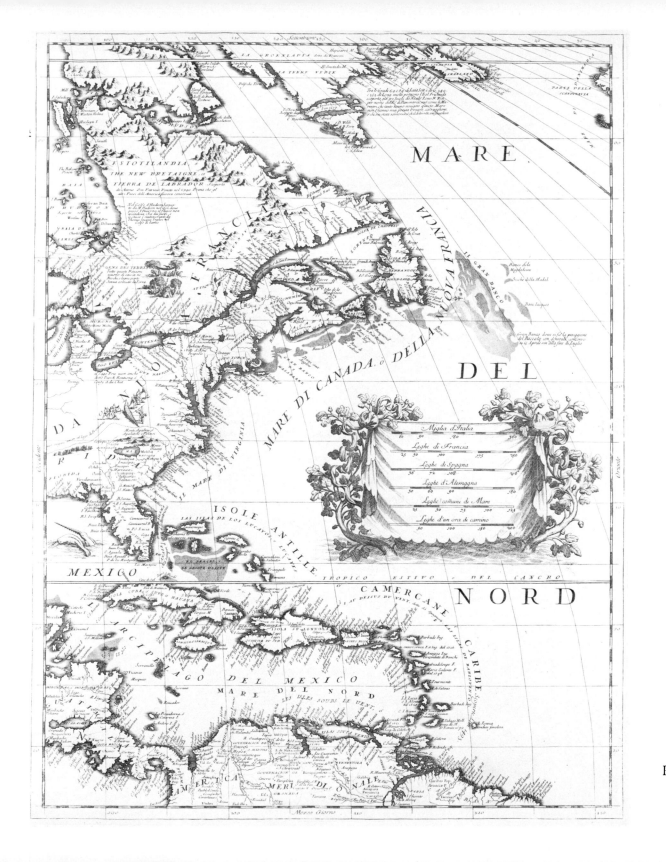

Plate 12.

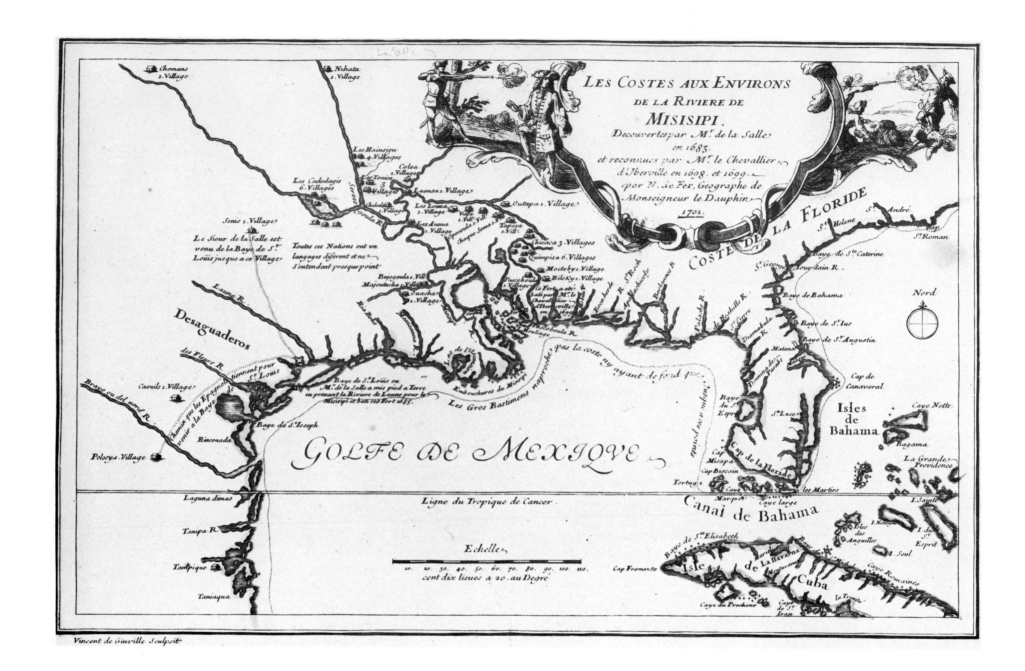

90

Plate 13. Nicolas de Fer, *Les Costes aux Environs de la Riviere de Misisipi. . . .*

Engraving: 21.5 × 33 cm (8.5 × 13 in.). Published in: Nicolas de Fer, *Atlas Curieux . . .* (Paris, 1700–1704).

The French experience in North America in the seventeenth and eighteenth centuries must be approached in the context of European rivalries. Map makers of the period, especially those working in the royal courts, reflected the politics of exploration, along with the legitimate demand for scientific information. Because of its magnitude and location, both geographically and politically, the Mississippi River played a significant role in the mapping of the continent.

Approaching the great river in the late seventeenth century from the north by land proved relatively easy, but determining the river's location by sea proved much more complex because scientists had not yet discovered a way to determine longitude with precision. Unlike latitude, which could be determined from celestial observations, longitude could be calculated only by dead reckoning, making the great number of rivers emptying directly into the Gulf of Mexico a challenge to explorers and distant map makers alike.

A French nobleman, René Robert Cavalier, Sieur de la Salle, reconnoitered the Mississippi from the north in 1682, claiming for France the lands the river drained. He returned to Paris and secured permission to establish a colony at the mouth of the Mississippi to formalize the French claim. When he returned he missed the Mississippi delta and landed on the Texas coast near Matagorda Bay, an error probably due to his inability to calculate longitude and because prominent maps of the period, such as one by Coronelli (Plate 12), grossly misjudged the location of the Mississippi, placing it far to the west of its true location. Nevertheless, La Salle established Fort Saint Louis in 1685 on the Texas coast, an act which greatly exacerbated France's rivalry with Spain in North America.

The significance bestowed on La Salle's adventures in the royal court of France was well illustrated in the works of the royal family's official geographer, Nicolas de Fer. *Les Costes Aux Environs de la Riviere de Misisipi,* issued in de Fer's *L'Atlas Curieux,* exhibited much more interest in ornamentation than recent French cartographic productions. But its primary purpose was clearly to show the progress the French were making in exploring their vast claim in North America, particularly in the explorations of La Salle and those of Pierre le Moyne, Sieur d'Iberville who, along with his brother Jean Baptiste, explored the coastlines of present-day Louisiana, Alabama, Mississippi, and Florida. The ornate cartouche graphically depicted the murder of La Salle in 1687.

Although de Fer contributed little new information on the Texas coastline or its interior, the map documented the knowledge of French officialdom of the areas claimed as part of Louisiana and, no doubt, added to the increasing resentment and fears on the part of the Spanish. Still unsettled was the question of whether the lands of the Tejas would be a part of New France or New Spain.

References: Lowery 251; Phillips, *Atlases* 532, 546; Day 1458.

The Collection of F. Carrington Weems, Houston, Texas.

Also as Color Plate II, p. 49.

Plate 14. Guillaume Delisle, *Carte du Mexique et de la Floride . . .* (Paris, 1703).

Engraving; 47.5 × 64.5 cm (18.8 × 25.3 in.).

Eugene C. Barker Texas History Center, University of Texas at Austin.

The shift of the center of the map trade from Amsterdam to Paris begun by Nicolas Sanson was completed by Guillaume Delisle, who elevated France from a competitive to a dominant position. Son of Claude Delisle, himself a geographer and pupil of Sanson, Guillaume Delisle was educated by the most illustrious mathematician and astronomer of his day, Jean Dominique Cassini. This training instilled in Delisle extremely high standards; he insisted on working from the most recent authorities and was unafraid to leave blank spaces in his maps when these were not available. As a result, his maps are characterized by a spare and clean appearance. He has often been cited as the first truly scientific cartographer, and his maps were widely copied by commercial ateliers of Paris, Amsterdam, and the rest of Europe. He was elected to the French Academy of Science in 1702 and in 1718 was named "Premier Geographe du Roi," a title created especially for him.

At the time Delisle prepared his map of Mexico and Florida, published in 1703 (Plate 14), much new information on the area had become available since Coronelli's effort fifteen years before (Plate 12). Firsthand reports from the survivors of La Salle's expedition, as well as from the French explorers and colonizers of the Gulf region like Bienville and d'Iberville, were carefully studied. Historian Carl Wheat called the result of Delisle's labors, the *Carte du Mexique et de la Floride*, "a towering landmark along the path of Western cartographic development." It was the first printed map to portray accurately the course and mouth of the Mississippi River. He correctly depicted the Great Lakes region, as well as the many English settlements along the East Coast. He also carefully set down the explorations of d'Iberville and his men on the Gulf Coast and the lower reaches of the Mississippi and Red rivers, and the Indian villages in East Texas where the Spanish constructed their missions and presidios. The present-day region of Texas and Oklahoma was portrayed as part of "Floride," a French possession, the name of which in later maps was changed to Louisiana. Delisle's placement of the Texas rivers is crude and inaccurate, showing many streams with strange, unrecognizable names debouching into "Bay St. Louis, which the Spaniards call St. Bernard." These faults probably resulted from Delisle's use of Spanish sources, the best available to him at the time.

Delisle's preeminence as a cartographer was such that his maps were in great demand and reprinted many times. He himself reissued the Mexico and Florida map in 1708, and in 1722 he made arrangements for it to be reprinted from a new plate by the Amsterdam publishers Jean Covens and Cornelius Mortier. Delisle's business was carried on by his wife after his death in 1726, and she entered into a partnership with one of his former students, Philippe Buache. In 1729 Bauche married Delisle's daughter and shortly thereafter assumed complete control of the firm. He was named "Premier Geographe du Roi" in 1729 and elected to the French Academy of Science in 1730. Buache reissued the 1703 map of Mexico and Florida, unchanged except for the addition of his own imprint, in 1745 (Plate 15). The map was issued for the last time in 1783, eighty years after its origin, by J. A. Dezauche who had assumed control of the business and styled himself as "successor of the Srs. Delisle and Philippe Buache."

Delisle's maps were pirated soon after they appeared and sold throughout Europe. His Royal Privilege, in the days before international copyright, availed him little protection. One of his most copied works was the map of Mexico and Florida. Many of these copies were fashioned in the Netherlands and the various German states. Matthew Seutter and his son-in-law Tobias Conrad Lotter both issued versions of the *Mexico et Floride* in Augsburg (Plate 18). Henri Chatelain and Pieter Schenk, working independently in Amsterdam, issued copies in 1719 and 1722 (Plate 16) respectively. Johann Baptist Homann also produced a copy of the famous Delisle work in Nuremberg in 1725 (Plate 17). All of these copies reproduced the geographical information contained in the Delisle map, but they abandoned the great French cartographer's plain, almost sterile style, for a much heavier, lavish, almost overpowering ornamentation characteristic of late Baroque period art. Opulent sea battles, ornate cartouches, and extravagant scenery were employed to fill the blank spaces that disturbed minds less scientific than Delisle's.

References: Plate 14: Wheat 84; Wagner, *Northwest Coast* 474; Phillips, *Atlases* 533; Bryan and Hanak 10; Tooley, *Delisle* 48–50; Lowery 256; Day 1489. Plate 15: Tooley, *Delisle* 52. Plate 16: Wheat 107; Lowery 198. Plate 17: Lowery 473; Day 385; Phillips, *Atlases* 586, 622. Plate 18: Lowery 328.

Plate 14 also as Color Plate III, p. 51.

Plate 15.   Guillaume Delisle, *Carte du Mexique et de la Floride . . .* (Paris, 1745).

Engraving; 47.5 × 64.5 cm (18.7 × 25.4 in.).

94

Plate 16. Peter Schenk, *Tabula Mexicae et Floridae . . .* (Amsterdam, 1722).

Engraving; 47×61 cm (18.5×24 in.).

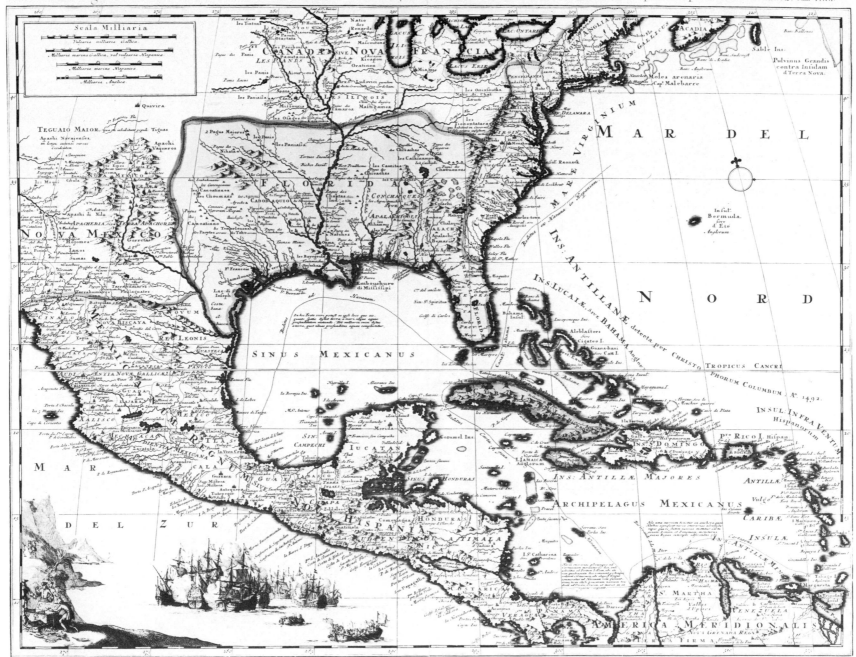

San Jacinto Museum of History, Houston, Texas.

Plate 17. Johann Baptist Homann, Regni Mexicani sea Novae Hispaniae . . . (Nuremberg, 1725?).

Engraving; 48 × 56.5 cm (18.9 × 22.3 in.).

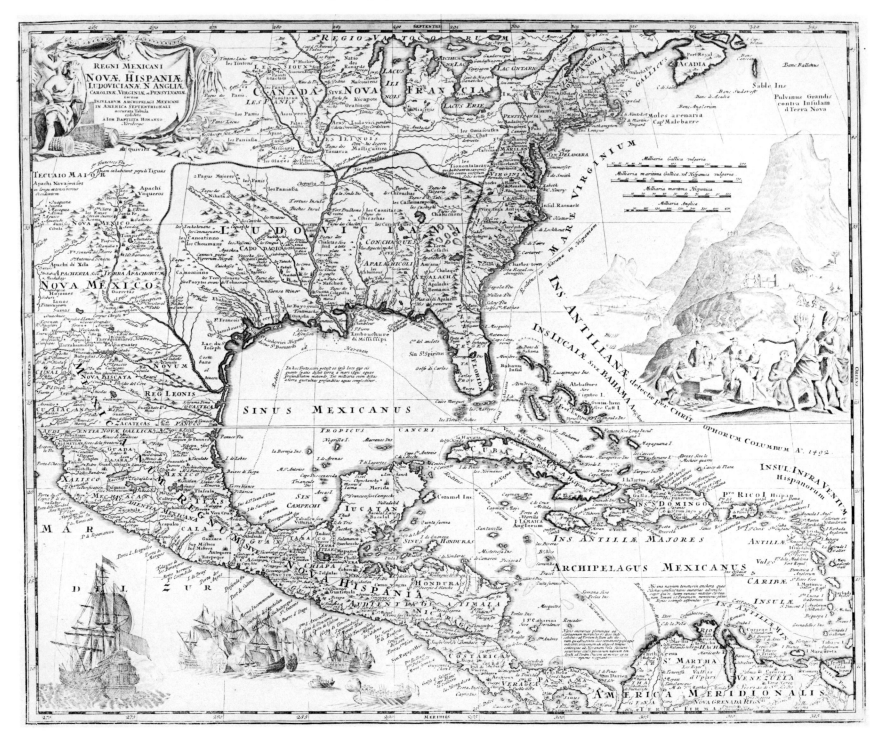

Collection of F. Carrington Weems, Houston, Texas.

Plate 18.   Tobias Conradus Lotter, *Mappa Geographica Regionem Mexicanam et Floridam . . .* (Augsburg, 1740).

Engraving; 47.5 × 57 cm (18.7 × 22.7 in.).

San Jacinto Museum of History, Houston, Texas.

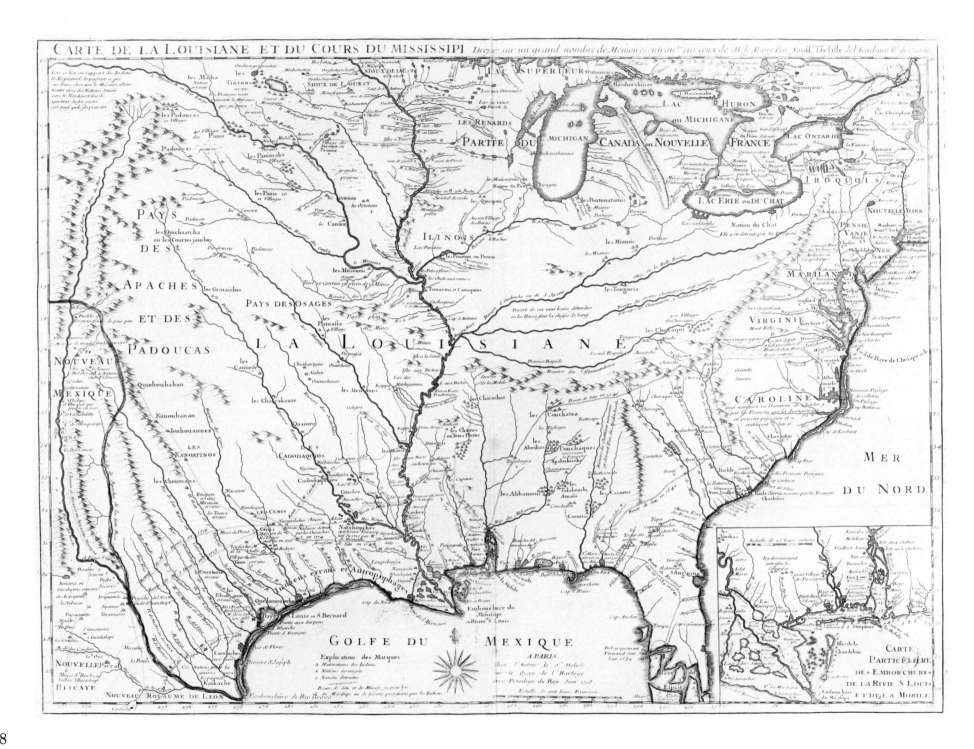

98

Plate 19. Guillaume Delisle, *Carte de la Louisiane et du Cours du Mississipi . . .* (Paris, 1718).

Engraving; 48.5 × 64.5 cm (19 × 25.4 in.).

During his most productive years, from 1700 until his death in 1726, Delisle produced over one hundred maps; scarcely a year passed without the production of a major new contribution. His most important achievement for North American cartography came in 1718, with the publication of his *Carte de la Louisiane et du Cours du Mississipi.* Because of its accurate information on the Mississippi and its tributaries, this map served throughout the eighteenth century as the prototype for most subsequent renderings of that great river. It was, moreover, a politically provocative map: what Delisle labeled Florida (Plate 14) in 1703 then appeared as the unmistakably French territory of Louisiana, stretching from the Rio Grande in the west to the Appalachians in the east. Angry protests from the British and Spanish governments against this cartographic usurpation were followed by a cartographic war, in which the map makers of each country issued productions showing their own territorial claims.

Politics aside, however, Delisle's rendering of Texas was a distinct improvement over previously published attempts. It featured an improved depiction of the river system and a much more accurate view of the coast. It also credibly delineated for the first time the land routes of all of the important explorers, including de Soto and Moscoso in 1540 and 1542, La Salle in 1687, and de Leon in 1689. Delisle's sources were also clearly revealed by the many references to St. Denis's explorations; the currency of his information was evident from the appearance of Natchitoches on the Red River, founded only the year before the map was printed. Throughout the map appeared the ranges of many Indian tribes and the locations of their villages, while boldly displayed along the Texas coast is the legend "nomadic and man-eating Indians," presumably referring to the Karankawa tribes that caused La Salle so much grief. The most important notation to Texas history, however, was that appearing along the Trinity: "Mission de los Tiejas, etablie in 1716." Referring to the earliest of the Spanish missions in East Texas, this phrase marked the first appearance of a form of the name *Texas* on a printed map, and thus Delisle has received proper credit for establishing Texas as a geographic place name.

Like his 1703 map of the region, Delisle's *Carte de la Louisiane* was widely plagiarized. It was copied outright in both English and Latin versions (with suitably altered legends and place names) within a year of its first appearance. Thereafter it was re-issued many times by the commercial publishers of Europe, sometimes with credit to Delisle, more often without. Variants of it continued to be issued, virtually unaltered, years after its author's death.

References: Wheat 99; Tooley, *Delisle* 43; Lowery 269, 284, 288; Kohl 238.

Sid Richardson Collection, Cartographic History Library, The University of Texas at Arlington.

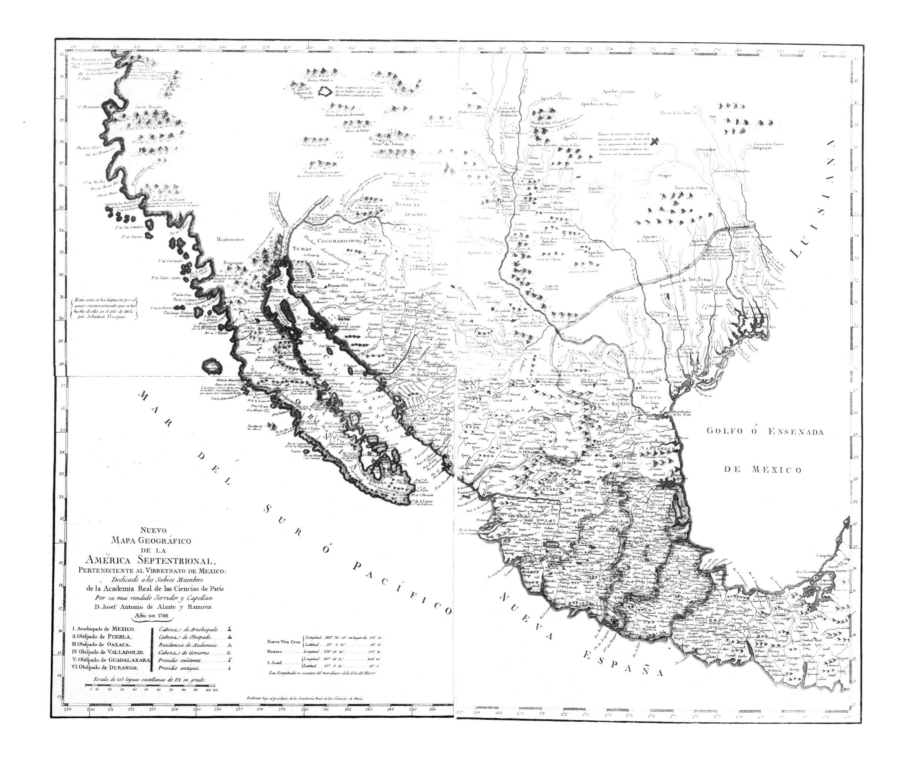

NUEVO
MAPA GEOGRÁFICO
DE LA
AMÉRICA SEPTENTRIONAL,
PERTENECIENTE AL VIRREYNATO DE MEXICO:
Dedicado á los Sabios Miembros
de la Academia Real de las Ciencias de París
Por su mui rendido Servidor y Capellan
D. Josef Antonio de Alzate y Ramirez.
AÑO DE 1768.

100

Plate 20. José Antonio Alzate y Ramírez, *Nuevo Mapa Geográfico de la America Septentrional . . .* (Paris, 1768).

Engraving; 54 × 64 cm (21.3 × 25.1 in.).

During the eighteenth century, the Enlightenment reached its peak in Europe. Stressing the potential for rational understanding of the world, the Enlightenment fostered a spirit of critical inquiry that developed into modern scientific method. In the colonies of Spain, a leading participant in Enlightenment activities was José Antonio Alzate y Ramírez, a Mexican-born cleric. Alzate had an insatiable curiosity about the world around him that was characteristic of the age. He made significant contributions to science in the fields of medicine, astronomy, mathematics, botany, and geography. He was elected to membership of the Royal Academy of Science in Paris, a distinctive honor for a Mexican colonial, and that august society published several of his papers. Alzate's stature as a man of learning was such that when the Mexican National Academy of Science was founded in 1884, it was called the Alzate Society.

In 1768 Alzate published a map of that part of North America which belonged to Spain, dedicated to his Fellows in the Royal Academy. As a prominent scientist, Alzate was given access to official information available in Mexico at the time, and he plainly based his map on reports and sketches of the expeditions of the early eighteenth century. Alzate depicted the interior of Mexico reasonably well, but in the Texas regions, as well as in the delineation of the West Coast, the map contained little detail and it was distorted in form. He displayed the rivers of Texas with a strict north-south orientation, rather than their true southeasterly direction. He completely omitted the Pecos River; the Nueces, with its tributaries the Frio and the Hondo, he showed as a minor branch of the Rio Grande. The Medina, actually a small tributary of the San Antonio River, was shown instead as the greatest river of the area, heading in the mountains east of Santa Fe and flowing into the Gulf of Mexico near the correct position of the Nueces. The Guadalupe was also extended and shown to flow into the Bay del Espíritu Santo without the waters of the San Antonio. The Colorado and the Brazos were shown as one. The Trinity, also greatly exaggerated, was drawn flowing across regions where the Arkansas and its branches actually run. He also gave the Red River a north-south orientation. Scattered villages of Apaches, and no other natural features, were all that was to be found in the area to the north of Texas.

As the only printed Spanish map of the area produced in the eighteenth century, Alzate's effort starkly illuminated the dearth of information available to the Spanish authorities concerning the interior provinces of New Spain, and a comparison with earlier productions like Delisle's document how little had been learned in the interim.

References: Wheat 149; Lowery 515, 516; Wagner, *Northwest Coast* 612.

Library of Congress, Washington, D.C.

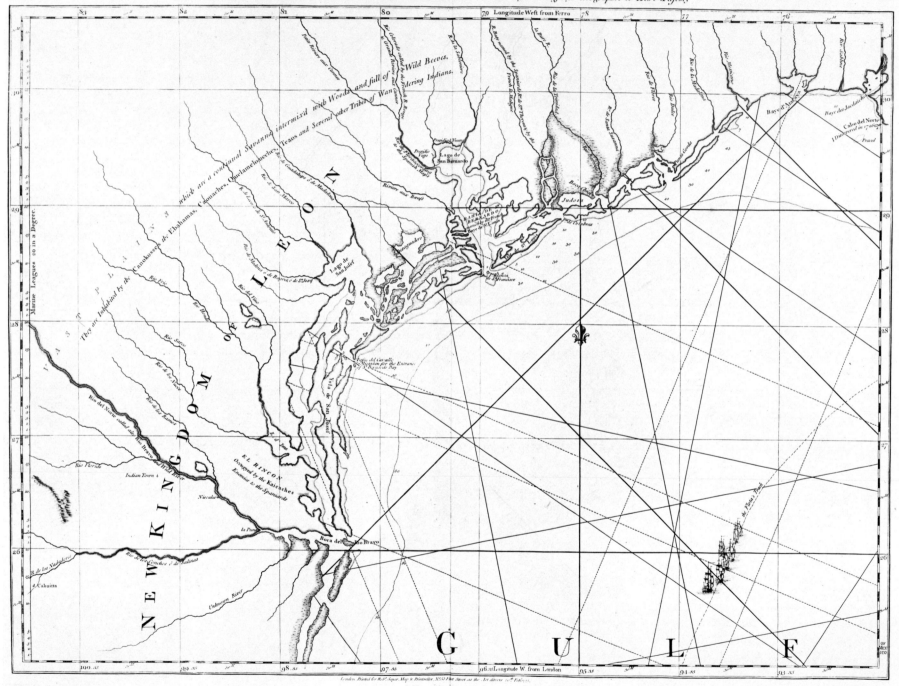

Plate 21. Thomas Jefferys, *The Western Coast of Louisiana and the Coast of New Leon.*

Engraving; 47 × 62 cm (18.5 × 24.4 in.). Published in: Thomas Jefferys, *West India Atlas . . .*
(London, 1775).

Britain's emergence in the eighteenth century as the world's dominant sea power was supported by London becoming the center for great advances in the cartographical sciences. One of the recognized leaders in the London group of map makers was Thomas Jefferys, whose talents earned him the title of Geographer to King George III.

Britain's keen interest in North America was reflected in Jefferys's well-known *American Atlas,* his *North American Pilot,* and his *West India Atlas,* in which he published this chart of the Texas coastline. Like other commercial map makers of the day, competition and overhead forced him to operate on a low budget, which often meant reliance on secondary sources and even plagiarism. But for his charts and maps depicting Spanish territories, however, Jefferys relied heavily on sketches and other maps captured by the British from Spanish warships.

Little is known of Jefferys's early life and training, but he was married in 1750 and, because throughout his adult life he listed himself as an engraver, it is likely that Jefferys entered the map business through the art of printing rather than through the science of geography. His career suffered a substantial setback when he went bankrupt in 1766, at which time Robert Sayer purchased a considerable portion of Jefferys's stock. It was, in fact, Sayer and his partner, John Bennett, who actually published some of Jefferys lasting contributions, including his *West India Atlas.* Before his death, Jefferys did publish more maps, with the aid of a young partner, William Faden.

This chart of the Texas coastline, although inaccurate, was the standard depiction of this area from the time of its publication in 1775 until the end of the century, when new Spanish surveys were published. Jefferys did show some interior cultural resources such as Indian villages and the site of La Salle's 1685 settlement, and the use of English, Spanish, and French nomenclature suggests the variety of his sources.

The lack of accurate information for this area is in part a reflection of the traditional secrecy of the Spaniards, but historically the map has remained an interesting and important documentation of the state of knowledge of the gateways to Texas.

References: Lowery 577; Phillips, *Atlases* 2699; Phillips, *Maps* p. 841; Day 1420, 2029; Streeter, *Texas* 1029n.

Amon Carter Museum, Ft. Worth, Texas.

Plates 22A & B.   Spain, Secretaria del Estado y de la Marina,
Carta Esférica que comprehende las costas del Seno Mexicano (Madrid, 1799).

Engraving; 60.5 × 93 cm (24.5 × 40.2 in.).

Spain, Dirección de Hidrografía, *Carta Particular de las Costas Setentrionales del Seno Mexicano . . .* (Madrid, 1807).

Engraving; 59 × 92 cm (23.2 × 36.2 in.).

In 1783 the interim governor of Spanish Louisiana, Bernardo de Gálvez, commissioned one of his lieutenants, José Antonio de Evia, to explore and map the entire northern coast of the Gulf of Mexico, from West Florida to Tampico. After a false start in 1783, Evia set out in 1785 and explored the coasts and bays of Florida, Alabama, Mississippi, Louisiana, Texas, and Mexico, reaching Tampico in September 1786. Along the way he explored San Bernardo Bay and took detailed soundings of Galveston Bay, which he named for his patron, who had by then been named the viceroy of Mexico.

More than a decade after Evia's careful explorations, his charts and sketches formed the basis for a new map of the Gulf Coast issued at the request of Don Juan Francisco de Langara y Huarte, the Spanish secretary of state and of the navy. Published in 1799, the *Carta Esférica que comprehende las costas del Seno Mexicano* represented an important advance in geographical knowledge and remained for many years the prototype for maps of the Gulf. In 1807, a larger-scale, slightly revised chart, showing only the coast between the Rio Grande and the Mississippi, was issued as the *Carta Particular de las Costas Setentrionales del Seno Mexicano. . . .* Like the *Carta Esférica* on which it is based, the *Carta Particular* was an improvement over the Jefferys chart (Plate 21),

which it superceded. It showed the mouths and lower courses of six of the seven most important rivers of Texas; the Brazos, though, was curiously absent. Detailed soundings of all of the coastal waterways were given. The Sabine River is shown as the boundary between Texas and Louisiana.

The chart was by no means perfect: the longitude of the major points, while internally consistent, are shown nearly a degree too far west, while the entire coastline north of the Nueces is given an exaggerated northward trend. In spite of these relatively minor errors, the *Carta Particular* is the first large-scale printed chart of the Texas coast based on actual soundings and explorations. The continued significance of the map was perhaps best indicated by the fact that nearly twenty years later, in 1825, the first president of the new Republic of Mexico, Guadalupe Victoria, ordered an exact copy printed and distributed.

References: Streeter, *Texas* 1029, 1041; Lowery 721, 744; Phillips, *Atlases* 4155.

Sid Richardson Collection, Cartographic History Library, The University of Texas at Arlington.

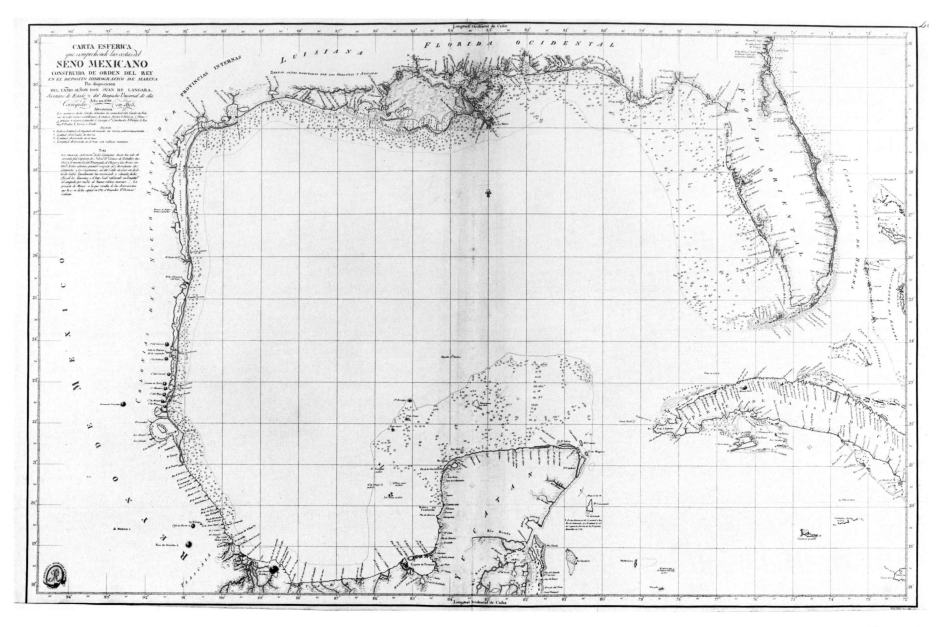

Plate 22A.

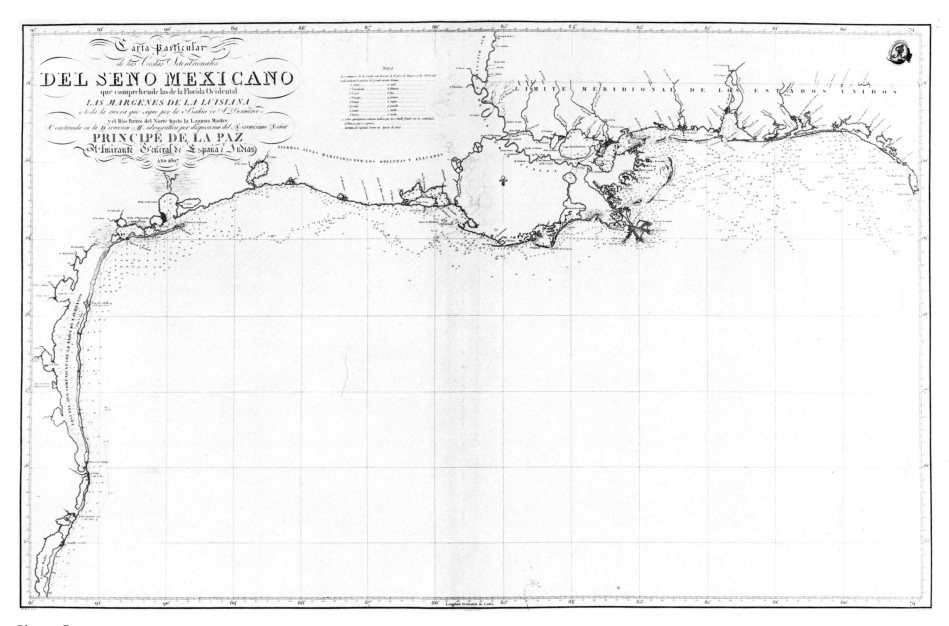

Plate 22B.

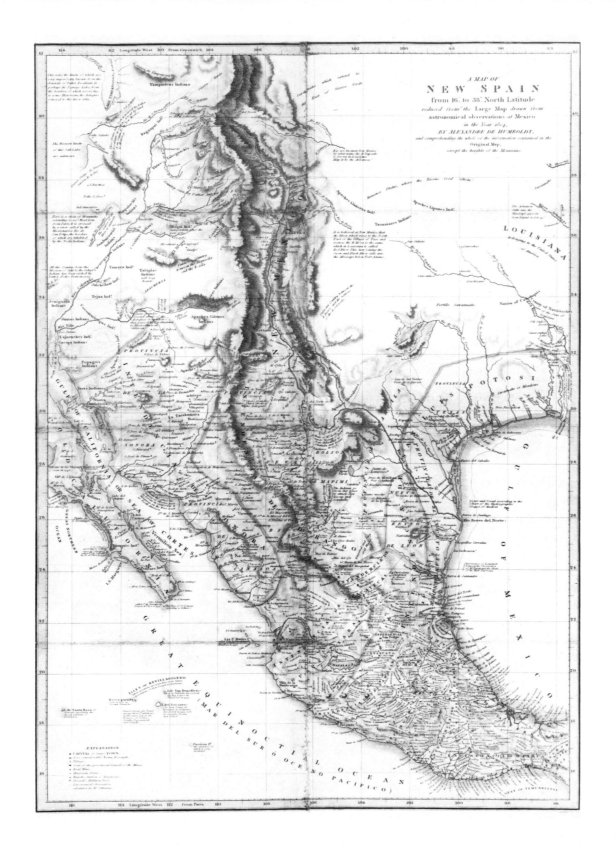

Plate 23.   Alexander von Humboldt, *A Map of New Spain....*

Engraving; 41.5×29 cm (16.3×11.4 in.). Published in: Alexander von Humboldt, *Political Essay on the Kingdom of New Spain* (London, 1811).

Alexander von Humboldt was, without question, the dominant scientific and philosophical figure of his age. Scion of a well-to-do family, Humboldt decided at an early age to devote his energies to science. After years of preparation at the best universities of Germany and experience in the German civil services, Humboldt embarked in 1799 on a five-year exploration of the New World to gather material for his scientific studies. Unlike all previous expeditions, financed by governments and either military or political in nature, Humboldt underwrote the expense of his journey himself and aimed only at the systematic scientific examination of the geography, flora, and fauna of the countries through which he traveled.

After completing a lengthy investigation of the South American continent, during which he made many important geographical and botanical discoveries, Humboldt spent nearly a year in Mexico. During this time he traveled and researched in the libraries and state archives of New Spain, preparing a detailed description of the area. Humboldt enjoyed the auspices of the Spanish government and was consequently privy to all of the confidential reports and information to be found in the records of the viceroyalty, and he began to assemble all of these materials for a new and accurate map of New Spain. This he prepared in draft, but like most of his endeavors, he left it to be completed on his return to Europe. On his way home in 1804, Humboldt spent three weeks visiting with President Thomas Jefferson and his secretaries, discussing his explorations and discoveries. While in Washington he made a copy of his map for the use of the United States government.

The map itself was finally completed in 1809 and published in the atlas to accompany Humboldt's *Essai Politique sur le Royaume de Nouvelle Espagne.* This work was one of the first to establish the field of geography as a modern science, and it was immediately translated into several European languages. The English version, with the map in a reduced format, was available in 1810.

In the *Essay* itself, Humboldt made several observations on the sources he used in compiling the map. He indicated that he followed the marine chart published by the Spanish hydrographic office in 1799 (Plate 22A) for the delineation of the coast of the Gulf of Mexico. Interestingly, Humboldt also averred that his depiction of the rivers of Texas was based on information given to him in Washington by Gen. James Wilkinson. His depiction repeated the error of Alzate and others in giving the rivers a southerly, rather than southeasterly, course. Humboldt compressed the western portion of the coastline while expanding the east, and in the space created between the Trinity and the Sabine he displayed two imaginary rivers. He showed the Brazos as a minor coastal stream and mislabeled the Lavaca as the Guadalupe, which he in turn left unnamed but showed correctly with its tributary, the San Antonio. The Pecos was shown, but placed too far west, falling far short of its actual origin in the mountains east of Santa Fe.

He showed Texas as a part of the Intendencia of San Luis Potosí, with a western boundary on the Nueces, curving around to the thirty-second parallel in the north. The eastern limits he depicted as east of the Rio Calcasieu in Louisiana, although he noted that this boundary was "not acknowledged by the Congress of Washington." Humboldt curiously misplaced the presidio of Nacogdoches to the location of the Orcoquisac presidio, and the missions of San Antonio were shown scattered throughout central Texas. Humboldt's map was probably the origin of the erroneous idea that the Guadalupe Mountains were east of the Pecos. To the north Humboldt made the common error of assigning the headwaters of the Canadian River in New Mexico to the Red River. On the other hand, he correctly surmised that the "Rio de Nepestle" was actually the great Arkansas River.

Humboldt's map has been termed a magnificent cartographic achievement, which in its depiction of the West it surely is. His depiction of the Texas regions, however, scarcely rates as an improvement over Alzate (Plate 20). His reliance on American sources, moreover, betrayed the scarcity of information in Mexico concerning the northeastern frontier of New Spain on the eve of Mexican independence.

References: Streeter, *Texas* 1042n; Wheat 273.

Eugene C. Barker Texas History Center, The University of Texas at Austin.

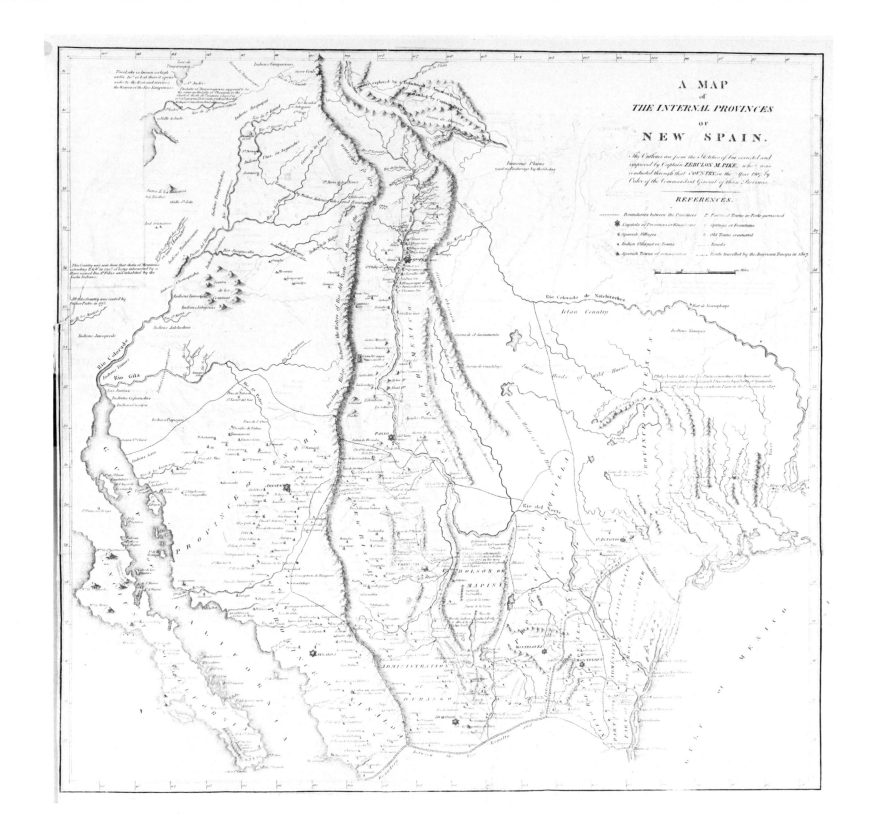

A MAP
of
THE INTERNAL PROVINCES
of
NEW SPAIN.

110

Plate 24. Zebulon Montgomery Pike, *A Map of the Internal Provinces of New Spain. . . .*

Engraving; 45 × 47 cm (17.7 × 18.5 in.). Published in: Zebulon Montgomery Pike, *An Account of Expeditions to the Sources of the Mississippi . . .* (Philadelphia, 1810).

Zebulon Montgomery Pike was a twenty-seven year old lieutenant in the United States Army when he left St. Louis, Missouri Territory, in July 1806, under orders from Gen. James Wilkinson, then Military Governor of the Louisiana Territory, to explore the headwaters of the Arkansas and Red rivers. Pike and his party proceeded overland to the Arkansas where, in the vicinity of present Great Bend, Kansas, a small party was detached under Lt. James Wilkinson, the general's son, to follow the river to its mouth. Pike and the remainder of the party continued up the Arkansas to the vicinity of present Pueblo, Colorado, and the mountain that now bears Pike's name. There they crossed over to the headwaters of the Rio Grande, where they were met and taken into custody by a detachment of Spanish troops and politely but firmly escorted south. In Chihuahua, Pike was quartered with the Louisiana-born Juan Pedro Walker, who was serving as an engineer in the Spanish army. Pike's papers were confiscated by the governor, and he and his men were escorted out of Spanish territory via Texas. Along the way they were handsomely entertained by Spanish officials in San Antonio, who seemed to treat the group as welcomed guests rather than dangerous interlopers.

Pike published an account of his adventures, including a description of Texas, which was one of the first detailed accounts published in English. The book contained a number of maps depicting Pike's route and discoveries, and one general map of the whole of New Spain. The work was published in Philadelphia in 1810, and not long thereafter Baron von Humboldt claimed publicly that Pike's map was a direct copy of the draft of his own large map that he had left in Washington. This copy of Humboldt's map (Plate 23) has unfortunately disappeared, making a direct comparison of the two impossible. There can be little doubt, however, that Pike did have access to Humboldt's draft after he returned to Washington and while he prepared his account; he probably did base much of his own map upon it. A comparison of Pike's map with Humboldt's final product, which was published in the same year, reveals little resemblance in the Texas portion.

Pike depicted Texas as a part of the Provincias Internas, which he described as being "independent of the Vice Roy." He showed a southern boundary at the correct location of the Nueces River, extending north-northwest to the Red River; interestingly, the boundary between Texas and the United States was left unmarked. Pike's delineation of the coast apparently followed the Jefferys model (Plate 21), rather than the superior *Carta Esférica* used by Humboldt. Pike's rendering of the rivers of Texas, on the other hand, was far superior to Humboldt's, probably benefiting not only from his own observations, but also with his brief association with Juan Pedro Walker. Pike showed the rivers with their correct southeasterly courses, and he avoided Humboldt's error of over-extending East Texas. He drew the Sabine and the Neches in their proper relationship and, although their lower courses were distorted to the east, they were shown draining into the same body of water, an unnamed Sabine Lake. Near the Trinity, which he delineated fairly accurately, is a "cantonment of 300 men" precisely at the correct location of the presidio of Orcoquisac. The Brazos River was, for the first time on a printed map, depicted in almost its proper length and shape; the Colorado, Guadalupe, and San Antonio were equally well presented. The unnamed Nueces, on the other hand, with its tributary the Frio (Cold Creek), he showed as a minor branch of the Rio Grande. In the west, Pike's rendering more nearly matched Humboldt's, with the Pecos flowing to the west of the "Sierra de Guadalupe," and with the headwaters of the Canadian again assigned to the Red. He curiously omitted the prominent peak that now bears his name.

In general, Pike's depiction of the Texas frontier was superior to Humboldt's in all but the details of the coast, and the portions that Pike undoubtedly borrowed from the Baron's model were the ones in which he is equally in error. Pike's map, unlike Humboldt's, was based primarily on firsthand reconnaissance, an element always present in the progress of geographic knowledge of the American West.

References: Streeter, *Texas* 1047; Wheat 299; Wagner-Camp 9; Day 450B.

Amon Carter Museum, Ft. Worth, Texas.

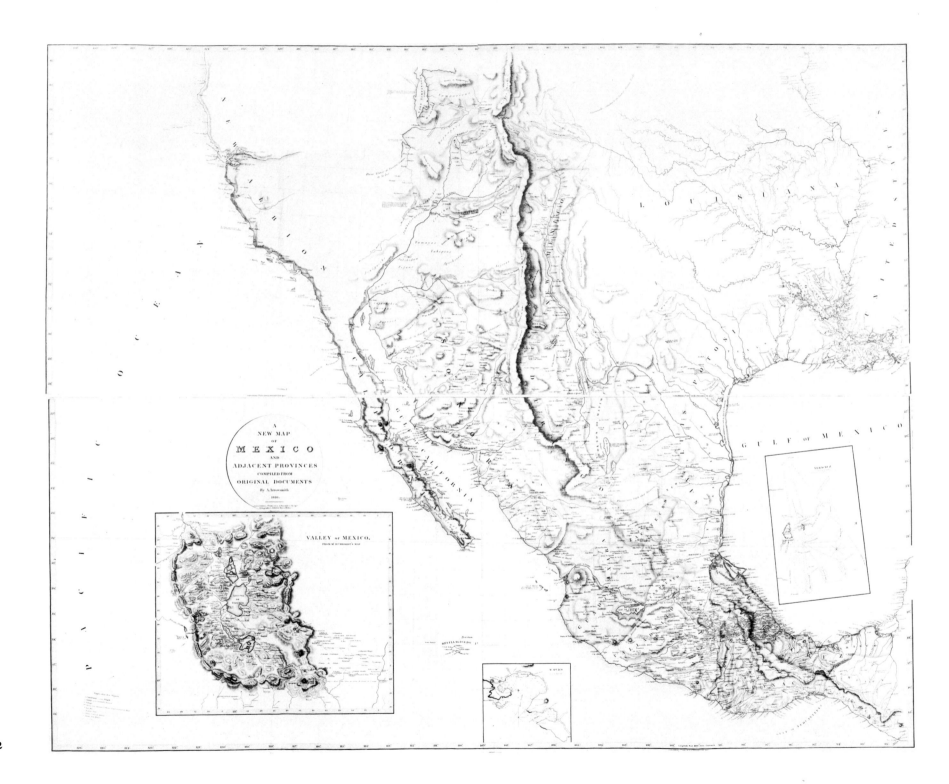

A NEW MAP OF MEXICO AND ADJACENT PROVINCES COMPILED FROM ORIGINAL DOCUMENTS By A. Arrowsmith

VALLEY OF MEXICO

Plate 25. Aaron Arrowsmith, *A New Map of Mexico. . . .*

Engraving; 129×158 cm (50.8×62 in.). Published in: Aaron Arrowsmith, *Atlas to Thompson's Alcedo*
(London, 1816).

Aaron Arrowsmith, Hydrographer to the King of England and Geographer to the Prince of Wales, was the most influential and respected map publisher of the first quarter of the nineteenth century. His maps were the result of careful synthesis rather than the systematic, scientific inquiry of Humboldt or military reconnaissance such as Pike's. His role in cartographic production was to gather the best information available from a wide variety of sources, weigh the relative merits of conflicting data, and compile from this the most accurate depiction possible of an area. Arrowsmith accomplished this synthesis better than any other commercial map maker of his day and, as a result, his maps were the most sought after and highly prized on three continents.

In 1810, the same year which witnessed the publication of Pike's narrative and the completion of the English translation of Humboldt's *Political Essay*, Arrowsmith published a large map of *Mexico and Adjacent Provinces*, covering the same area as Humboldt's map. The Baron later bitterly charged that Arrowsmith's map was a blatant plagiarism of his own. There can be little doubt that Arrowsmith, like Pike, leaned heavily on Humboldt for his depiction of the Mexican interior; there was, to be sure, no better source from whom to borrow. Arrowsmith's map was, however, no mere copy. Relying on information provided to him by the Hudson's Bay Company, he added significant details in the Northwest and his depiction of the California coast was probably taken from the British explorer Vancouver's own charts. In the Texas area he undoubtedly used Pike's rendition of the rivers, particularly of the Brazos and the Guadalupe, while he followed Humboldt in tracing the coast from the Spanish hydrographic office chart. Consequently, true to his form, by combining the best parts of Humboldt's and Pike's maps and avoiding their errors, and by adding his own new information, Arrowsmith contributed a significantly improved depiction of the region, thereby adding to a well-deserved reputation for excellence.

References: Streeter, *Texas* 1046; Wheat 295; Phillips, *Maps* p. 408.

Christensen/Byram Collection, Austin, Texas.

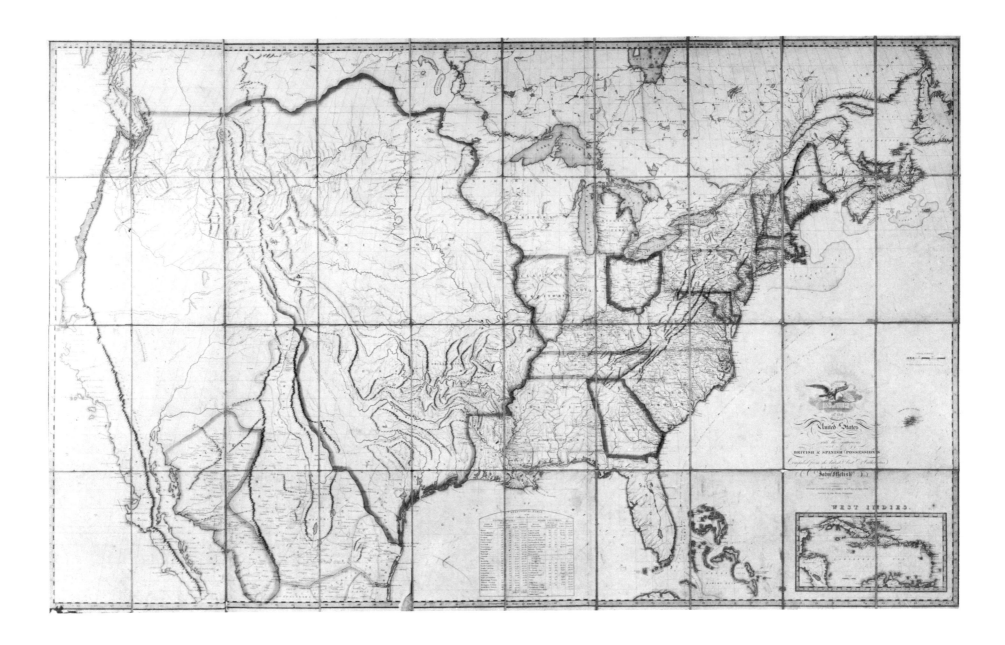

Plate 26.   John Melish, *Map of the United States . . .* (Philadelphia, 1816).

Engraving; 87 × 143 cm (34 × 56.3 in.).

Independence for the British colonies in North America created a new political division of these rich lands, but it also began a process of severing economic ties, including the commercial map trade. Early in the nineteenth century, Philadelphia emerged as a center for printing and map making, and the purchase of Louisiana from France in 1803 brought to the foreground the question of the westward extent of Louisiana. It also stimulated an intense push westward among land-hungry settlers hoping to take advantage of cheap virgin lands.

The United States and Spain finally came to terms in the Adams-Onís Treaty in 1819, in which the United States relinquished its claim to Texas in favor of a boundary following the Sabine, Red, and Arkansas rivers to the forty-second parallel. In exchange for this concession, Spain agreed to turn over its claims in Florida. Many Americans had already settled in Texas, claiming that the true boundary of Louisiana extended as far west as the Rio Grande, resulting in later years in a movement demanding the "reannexation" of Texas.

The division of these lands in the Adams-Onís Treaty was facilitated by the use of a popular and widely disseminated map by John Melish, a Philadelphia publisher who had established the first enterprise in the United States exclusively devoted to the publication of geographies and maps. Recognizing that the demand for geographical information on the American West was limitless in the foreseeable future, Melish undertook to accumulate a vast amount of descriptions, statis-

tics, and maps, and in 1816 produced in six sheets his famous map. It proved so popular that it was reprinted at least twenty-two times by the end of 1822. For the Texas area, Melish relied heavily on the surveys conducted by William Darby, who had personally surveyed much of the Sabine River area. Melish had published Darby's work separately in 1816 as a *Map of the State of Louisiana*, accompanied by the *Geographical Description of the State of Louisiana*. Melish's maps significantly improved the descriptions and depictions of the Texas interior, but perhaps its most lasting value to history was its official association with the Adams-Onís Treaty. Because Melish's 90th meridian, today the eastern boundary of the Texas Panhandle, was off by approximately ninety miles, controversy and court litigation concerning the correct boundary lasted well beyond Texas's annexation. Moreover, Melish's map graphically conveyed the controversy in the United States over the boundary of Texas and Louisiana. Of lasting value, too, was the widespread dissemination of new information concerning Texas geography only five years before Stephen F. Austin decided to honor his father's contract with the Mexican government to bring in Anglo-American settlers to inhabit this rich new land.

References: Streeter, *Texas* 1057; Wheat 322; Streeter, *Sale* 3797 ff.; Risto, *Melish.*

Eugene C. Barker Texas History Center, The University of Texas at Austin.

A MAP OF MEXICO LOUISIANA
AND THE
MISSOURI TERRITORY
including also
THE STATE OF MISSISSIPPI, ALABAMA TERRITORY, EAST & WEST FLORIDA, GEORGIA, SOUTH CAROLINA
by
JOHN H. ROBINSON, M.D.

PACIFIC OCEAN

GULF OF MEXICO

SOUTH SEA

116

Plate 27. John Hamilton Robinson, *A Map of Mexico, Louisiana, and the Missouri Territory . . .* (Philadelphia, 1819).

Engraving; 169 × 195 cm (66.5 × 76.8 in.).

When Zebulon Pike set out from St. Louis to explore the West in July 1806, in his party was a man his own age who he described in his journal as "a young gentlemen of science and enterprise"—John Hamilton Robinson. Robinson served as the medical officer of the expedition and was an important force within it; he has been called the *de facto* leader. It has even been suggested that Robinson wrote most of Pike's *Account*, since there are striking similarities to his own. Robinson accompanied Pike throughout his adventures, and with Pike made the acquaintance of the enigmatic Mexican officer, Juan Pedro Walker. After returning to the United States with Pike, Robinson again made several journeys to Mexico, where he associated with the republican forces of revolt and was appointed brigadier general in their forces. By 1818, on one of his trips back to the States, Robinson issued a prospectus for a map of Mexico and Louisiana, to be sold on subscription. This map appeared in 1819, shortly before Robinson's death in Natchez, at the age of forty.

The map showed most of North America, and on its face Robinson asserted: "The Information on which the author feels himself justified in the publication of this Map, is from his own knowledge of the Country in his several voyages thither and also the several Manuscript Maps which are now in his possession, drawn by order of the Captain General of the Internal Provinces and Viceroy of Mexico." At least one of these official drafts he must have procured from Juan Pedro Walker, for he credited that officer with his delineation of the West Coast. What other information he received from that source is open to conjecture. Robinson himself was either intimately acquainted with the region he portrayed or was close to associates who were, for the face of the map was scattered with personal observations, such as the notation "Excellent wines made here" near El Paso. The map was perhaps the best then available in its depiction of the Sabine and Red rivers, but the information on the coast was as erroneous as Pike's. The delineations of the rivers of Texas, aside from the Sabine, also resembled Pike's and indicated that Robinson probably had little firsthand knowledge of Texas. The eastern boundary of Texas followed the Sabine to the thirty-second parallel, and then curiously followed that line due west to the 103rd meridian, thus assigning all of present North Texas to New Mexico.

Much of Robinson's cartography in the West is apocryphal, or based on outdated models. He continued to confuse the source of the Canadian with the Red, and he showed numerous imaginary mountain ranges. His depiction of the headwaters of the Arkansas and the Rio Grande echoed Pike, but unlike that explorer, he prominently displayed the great mountain peak which he and Pike discovered and measured, and for the first time he assigned it the name of his well-known associate.

The most significant feature of the Robinson map was political. He carefully set forth the conflicting boundary claims of the United States and Spain to the Louisiana Territory, showing Spain's claim to most of the Mississippi Valley, and the United States's claim to the Rio Grande and thence north. In between he highlighted the compromise boundary established that very year in the Adams-Onís Treaty, and thus illuminated graphically for the first time the territories in question. Many Americans preferred to focus on what they had given up rather than what they had gained, and Robinson's map is thus an interesting glimpse at the region on the eve of Anglo colonization.

References: Streeter, *Texas* 1073; Wheat 334.

Sid Richardson Collection, Cartographic History Library, The University of Texas at Arlington.

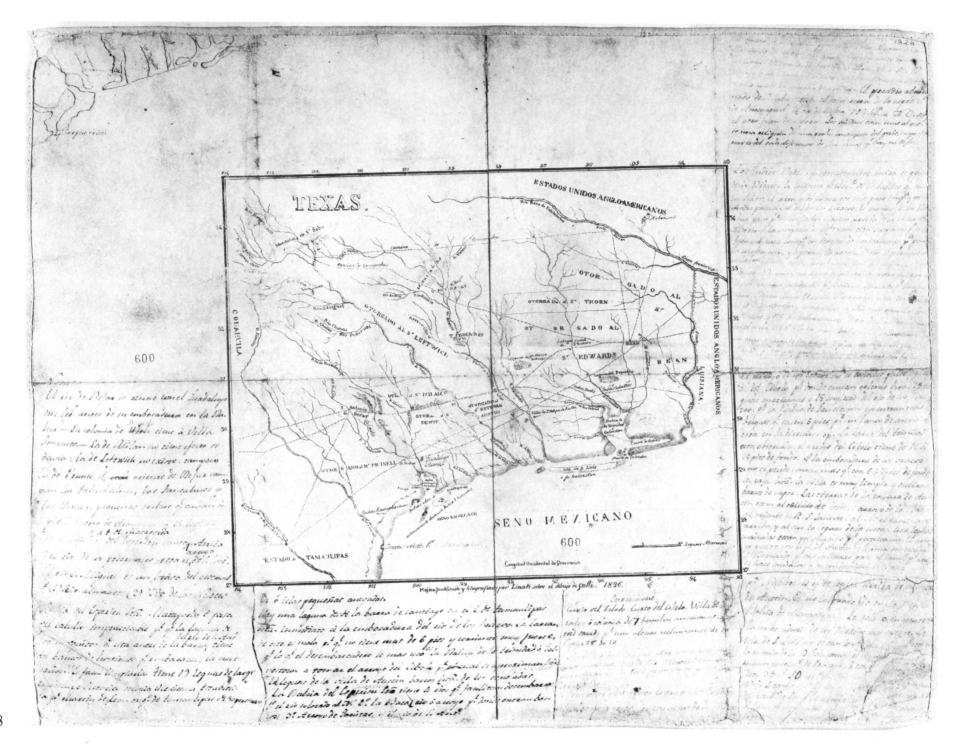

Plate 28.   Fiorenzo Galli, *Texas . . .* (Mexico, 1826).

Lithograph; 23 × 28 cm (9.1 × 11 in.).

The introduction of lithography into Mexico has generally been credited to Claudio Linati. He arrived in that country in 1825 and, together with a friend, Fiorenzo Galli, began publishing a pocket-size magazine illustrated with hand-colored lithographs under the title *El Iris*. In addition, Linati lithographed numerous separate plates and prints, among them a sketch map executed by Galli in 1826, which holds the distinction of being the first printed map of Texas.

The map bears some resemblance to Stephen F. Austin's 1822 manuscript sketch, many copies of which he is known to have executed in the Mexican capital during his stay in 1822 and 1823. The names "Punta Pecan" on the Red River and "Seno Lovelace" in the Gulf seem to be taken directly from Austin's draft. Galli's map showed Texas bounded on the east and the north by the Sabine and the Red Rivers respectively, and on the west by the Nueces. The depiction of the coast was particularly advanced for the period, although the details of Matagorda Bay were lacking. The rivers of the area were shown more accurately than ever before on a printed map. The Brazos and the Trinity were both shown to their full extent, and the upper courses of these streams, as well as the Colorado, were delineated in great detail. The Neches, on the other hand, was curiously absent, and the San Antonio still entered its bay separately from the Guadalupe. The land grants of Bean, Thorn, Leftwich, Austin, DeWitt, Milam, and Prunell were all shown with their boundaries, and the sites of the important *villas* and missions were laid down as well.

Only one known copy of the map exists, preserved in the Barker Texas History Center at The University of Texas at Austin. Its wide margins are filled with manuscript notations in the hand of Manuel Mier y Terán, who came to Texas in 1828 as the commander of the commission to establish the boundary between the United States and Mexico. Presumably Terán had the map with him at the time and the notes represent his observations in the field. They add substantially to the geographical information conveyed by the map.

The notes deal with many different topics, including the status of the various colonial ventures, the true locations and courses of several streams, and the various Indian tribes and problems concerning them. Extensive notes deal with the navigability of some of the bays and rivers and the locations of additional settlements. Many of these features he noted on the face of the map as well and indicate a thorough knowledge of the geography of the region. Terán is known to have exchanged information with Austin, and it is interesting to speculate what was contributed by whom.

References: Streeter, *Texas* 713; Castañeda, *Three Manuscript Maps;* McLean, *Papers* II:457.

Eugene C. Barker Texas History Center, The University of Texas at Austin.

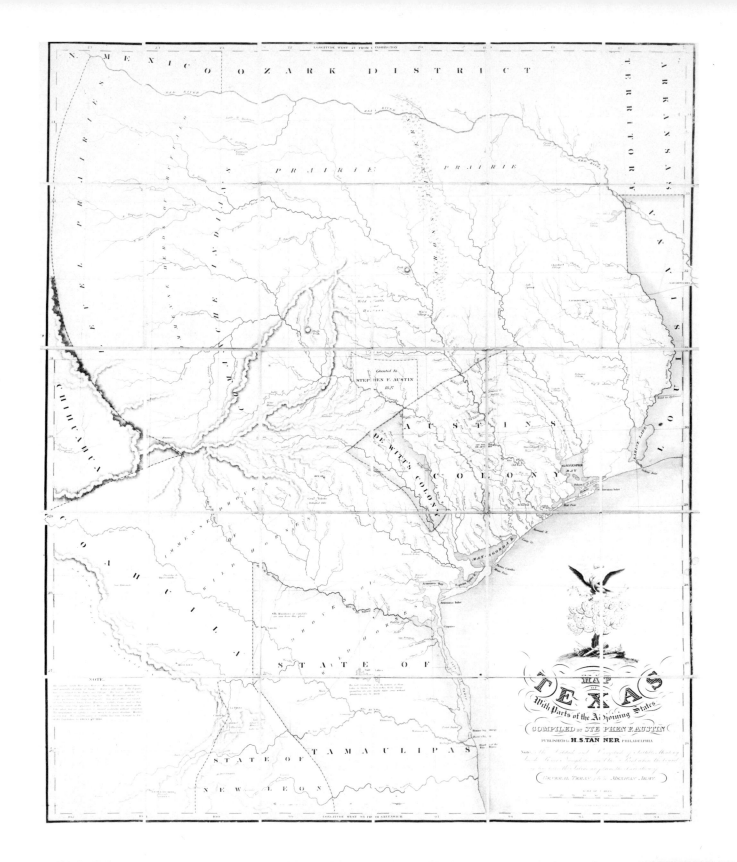

120

Plate 29. Stephen Fuller Austin, *Map of Texas* . . . (Philadelphia, 1830).

Engraving; 74 × 60 cm (29 × 23.6 in.).

During the many months Stephen F. Austin spent in Mexico in 1822 and 1823 seeking confirmation of his father's colonization grant, he presented numerous petitions to the successive governments coming to power in that turbulent time. In every one of these documents Austin stressed the urgent necessity for compiling a good map of Texas, a task he pledged to undertake upon the confirmation of his grant. After returning to Texas in 1823 with a special congressional decree authorizing his colonizing venture, Austin set to work fulfilling the terms of his grant, and he did not forget his pledge to make a map of the province. He spent the next six years gathering information from travelers and surveyors and combined this with his own observations detailing the territory he was trying to map. During this period he prepared numerous sketches, plats, and preliminary drafts, many of which have been preserved in his papers. During 1828, as he accelerated his work on the map itself, he made arrangements through his attorney and kinsman in Philadelphia, Thomas F. Leaming, to have the map printed and distributed by the prominent Philadelphia publisher, H. S. Tanner. Finally in the summer of 1829, Austin was satisfied with the detail of his work; he forwarded a manuscript draft of the finished map to Tanner in June, and the following month dispatched a Spanish copy to the Mexican government, fulfilling his long-standing promise.

Tanner carefully engraved the plate for the map and issued it in March 1830. It was immediately in high demand, and Tanner reissued it four times before the end of the decade. It was without question the most accurate depiction of the area to date, and it served as a model for many subsequent productions. Austin showed Texas bounded on the southwest by the Nueces; from the headwaters of that stream the western boundary followed a broad arc northeast to the Red River. The eastern boundary was shown as the Sabine to the thirty-second parallel, thence due north to the Red, which served as the northern boundary. The map showed both of Austin's grants as well as DeWitt's, but no other grants were shown. The map recorded the old settlements of San Antonio, Nacogdoches, and Goliad, and the roads connecting them, and it also portrayed for the first time on a printed map the new towns of San Felipe de Austin, Harrisburg, Brazoria, Matagorda, Victoria, and Gonzalez. Austin set down the rivers accurately and in great detail, and the rendition of the coast significantly improved previously published attempts. The map pointed out locations of Indian tribes, "immense herds of buffalo," and "immense droves of wild horses," as well as labeling prominent ridges and the crosstimbers.

In the letter that accompanied the Spanish draft to Mexico, Austin stated that his purpose in compiling the map "has been to add to the fund of geographic knowledge of Mexican territory, and to make known our beloved Texas . . . to the Mexicans and to the world. . . ." Although these patriotic reasons were no doubt a part of Austin's motivation, other factors were certainly involved as well. In a later letter to Leaming, Austin discussed in detail the rationale for his cartographic endeavors. After echoing the above sentiments, in which he claimed that the object of making the map was "to bring this country into the public view, for it has been literally buried in obscurity up to the last year," Austin embarked on a thorough discussion of the history of his involvement with Texas, the growing Mexican unease and mistrust of Anglo colonization, and their later attempts to restrict or halt it. Austin indicated that he decided that some quiet promotion was necessary to defeat Mexican restrictions and insure the success of the colonies. In a completely candid observation he concluded: "I determined to have the Map published as the Most effectual means of operating on an intelligent people, and the least dangerous with the Mexicans, for not many of them know anything about maps. . . ."

References: Streeter, *Texas* 1115; Bryan and Hanak 21.

San Jacinto Museum of History, Houston, Texas.

Also as Color Plate IV, p. 53.

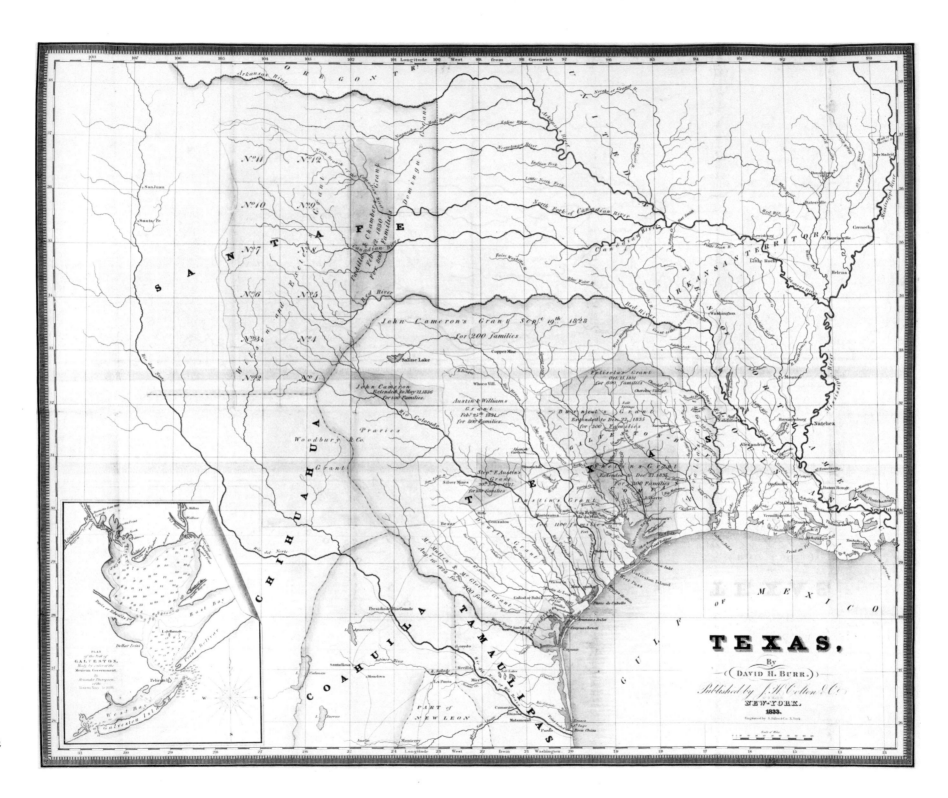

TEXAS,

By

DAVID H. BURR.

Published by J. H. Colton & Co.

NEW-YORK.

1833.

122

Plate 30. David H. Burr, *Texas* (New York, 1833).

Engraving; 54 × 42 cm (21.3 × 17 in.).

Anglo-Americans in the early decades of the nineteenth century reacted quickly to the opportunities to settle in the rich lands made available to them through empresario contracts in the Mexican state of Coahuila y Texas. Stephen F. Austin's 1830 map of Texas (Plate 29), showing his two grants and one to Green DeWitt, aroused great interest in Texas, both on the part of potential settlers as well as in the American government itself. In 1833, the Geographer to the United States House of Representatives, David Burr, updated Austin's earlier effort with a new map of Texas showing seventeen land grants, including those to Wilson and Exter, Dominguez, Padilla and Chambers, Cameron, Woodbury and Company, McMullen and McGloin, Powers, de Leon, DeWitt, Burnet, Vehlein and de Zavala, and Filisola. Significantly, Burr's map was the first large-scale map of Texas to show claims to lands north of the Arkansas River, and with the inclusion of the new land grants, his map documented the explosion of immigration into Texas.

Burr's map also included the "Plan of the Port of Galveston" drawn by Alexander Thompson, a citizen of the United States who served in the Mexican Navy in the 1820s. In 1828 the Mexican government commissioned him to chart the coast of Galveston Island, a charge which resulted in this map of Galveston Bay.

Rather than following the line drawn in the Treaty of 1819, delineating the western boundary of Louisiana, Burr's map showed the Texas boundary some twenty miles west of the intersection of the Sabine River with the thirty-second parallel, an error which later led to litigation between Arkansas and Texas. Burr's map was also the first printed effort to show the grants of Stephen Wilson and Richard Exter in the present-day Texas Panhandle area.

The map was reprinted in 1834 and in 1835 with only slight modifications, and again in 1845, showing Texas as a state in the Union. As a geographer Burr is perhaps best remembered for his 1839 *American Atlas*, but his cartographic productions of Texas, now quite rare, served as a reputable chronicle of the progress made in the discovery of modern Texas.

References: Streeter, *Texas* 1134; Bryan and Hanak 22.

Collection of Paul G. Bell, Houston, Texas.

Also as Color Plate V, p. 55.

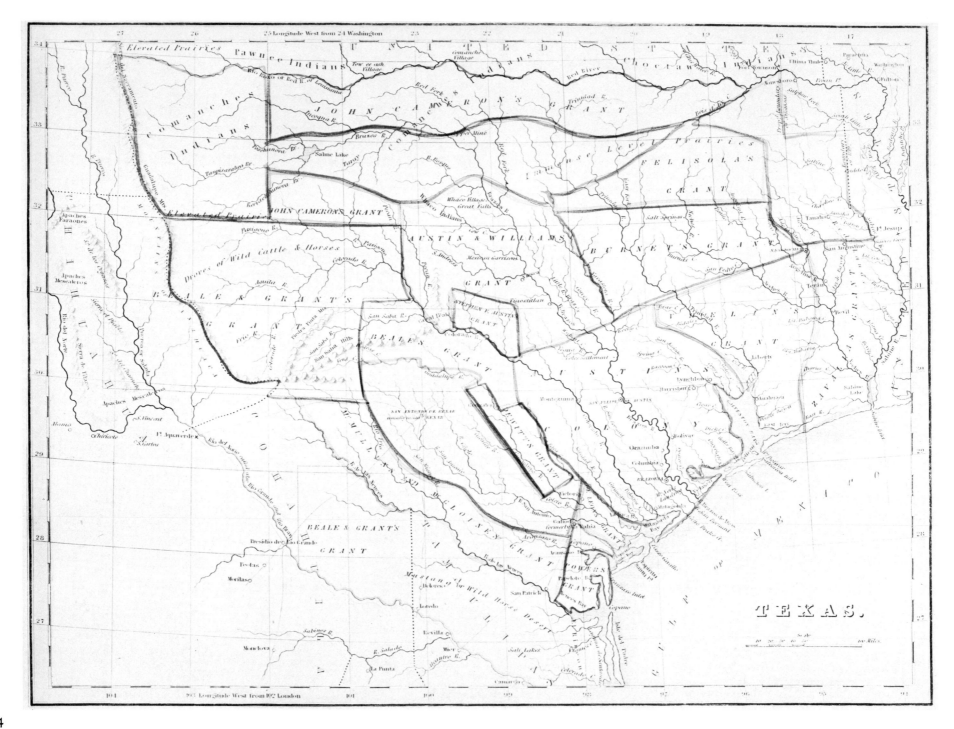

TEXAS.

124

Plate 31.   Thomas Gamaliel Bradford, *Texas.*

Engraving; 20 × 27 cm (8 × 10.5 in.). Published in: Thomas Gamaliel Bradford, *A Comprehensive Atlas,*
Geographical, Historical and Commercial (New York, 1835).

Although Thomas Gamaliel Bradford was not a leading figure in the nineteenth century American map trade, his atlases are significant to the cartographic history of Texas because they included the first two maps to depict Texas as an independent republic.

Bradford's first of three works, *A Comprehensive Atlas . . . ,* has survived in at least four variant forms, all dated 1835, but some clearly published later. The first of these was issued by the well-known Boston printer W. D. Ticknor, and contained no map of Texas. It must have sold well, for late that same year, or early the next, another edition was issued by the American Stationers's Company. In this issue Bradford, aroused by the revolutionary events in Texas that led to conflict, inserted a new map of Texas after the one of Mexico, and accompanied it with a two-page text describing Texas as "at present engaged in an arduous struggle for independence." The text included a complete geographical description of the province, its rivers and harbors, its colonies and towns, its climate, crops, and natural resources. It also included a brief account of the colonial developments, leading up to the Declaration of Causes that initiated the Texas Revolution in November 1835. After quoting clauses of this declaration, the account concluded: "It is needless to enter into the details of what followed, as they are fresh in the minds of all."

The map itself appeared to be copied directly from Austin's (Plate 29), the only readily available authority. The depiction of the rivers and the coast were certainly modeled from Austin's, as were the numerous notes on its face relating to Indian tribes and horse herds. The map differed from Austin's primarily in its prominent display of numerous colonization grants and a plethora of new settlements and towns, indicative of the massive influx of colonists occurring after the publi-

cation of Austin's work. Another significant departure from Austin was the map's depiction of the Arkansas boundary controversy. The "Boundary of 1819" was shown, corresponding to the present boundary of the state, but to the west another line, labeled "prop'd Boundary of Arkansas," was depicted, which would have assigned the northeast corner of Texas to that state. The map also extended west beyond Austin's to the Pecos, erroneously showing the Guadalupe Mountains to the east of that river.

Two later editions of Bradford's *Atlas* appeared, both still dated 1835 on the title page, with differing editions of the map and the text on Texas. The first of these, which must have appeared in late 1836, carried the map unaltered, but with the text compressed to one page and referring to Texas as an independent nation. The final form of the *Atlas* left this new text unaltered, but the map was changed to show the inchoate counties and land districts of the young Republic. Bradford published a completely new atlas in 1838, in a larger format, and the map of Texas it contained was even more clearly patterned on Austin's.

Aside from showing Texas as a separate state, the maps and text Bradford inserted into his atlases are historically important for clearly demonstrating the demand in the United States for information about Texas during the Revolution and the early years of the Republic. They also serve to confirm the importance of Austin's map as a source for that information.

Reference: Phillips, *Atlases* 770.

Sid Richardson Collection, Cartographic History Library, The University of Texas at Arlington.

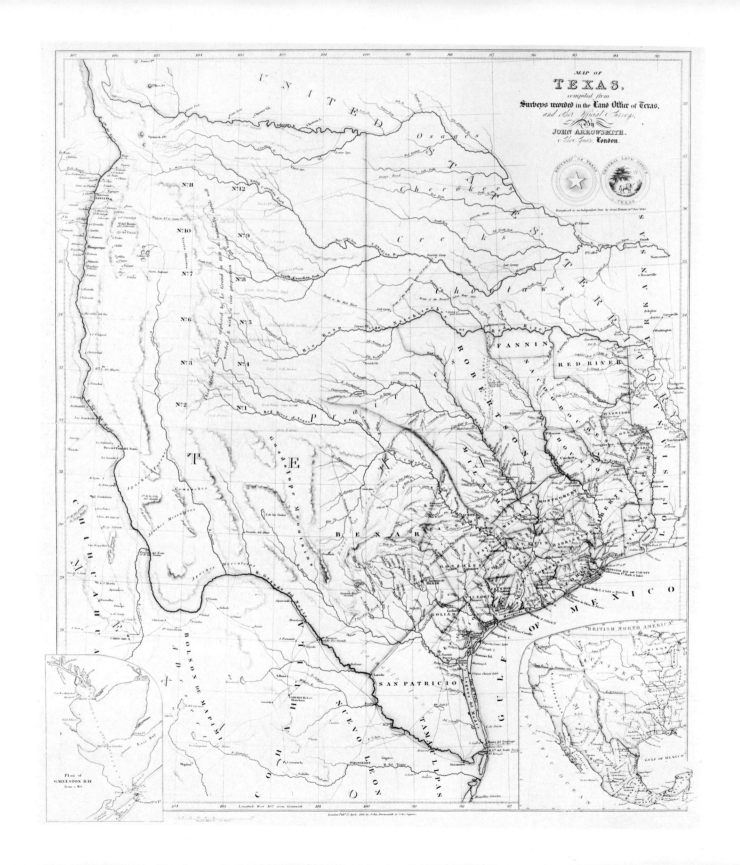

Plate 32. John Arrowsmith, *Map of Texas* (London, 1841).

Engraving; 61 × 50 cm (24 × 19.7 in.).

By the time of the new Republic of Texas emerged in 1836, Great Britain had become the leading center of commerce and industry, with London developing as the primary center for map production. One of the most famous London map makers, Aaron Arrowsmith, set high standards in his scientific approaches in map making. After his death in 1823, he was ultimately succeeded in the trade by his nephew, John Arrowsmith, who had studied and worked under him. Beginning in 1834, John Arrowsmith continued the tradition of excellence established by his uncle, issuing some of the finest cartographic productions of his time.

In 1841 Arrowsmith issued his now famous *London Atlas*, which contained a new map of the Republic of Texas. Its up-to-date information included an accurate depiction of boundaries and river system and the latest developments in its political divisions. The second edition of this map was included in a popular travel book by William Kennedy, *Texas: The Rise, Progress and Prospects of the Republic of Texas*, also printed in 1841.

Arrowsmith's map was probably the first to show the full extent of Texas's claim to the region of the upper Rio Grande, an area included within Texas's boundaries until the Compromise of 1850. It was issued with two insets, one showing the geographical relationship of Mexico, Texas, and the United States, and another inset showing Galveston Bay, with soundings illustrating for the traveler the best route to the new city of Houston. The popularity and general acceptance of the map has been documented by the fact that many map makers copied liberally from Arrowsmith's map, including some of its errors. For example, a number of later maps continued Arrowsmith's statement printed in the western, arid region of Texas that "this tract of Country explored by LeGrande in 1833 is naturally fertile well wooded, & with a fair proportion of water." As one of the earliest maps to contain information from the General Land Office of Texas, the map located Indian tribes, major roadways, and included editorial comments for the benefit of the future traveler to Texas, such as "excellent land," "valuable land," "rich land," and "delightful country."

In spite of its few errors, the map certainly was the best information on Texas geography available in Europe during a decade in which the political fate of the new Republic was of international concern.

References: Streeter, *Texas* 1373; Wheat 451; Phillips, *Atlases* 764.
Collection of Mr. and Mrs. Jenkins Garrett, Ft. Worth, Texas.

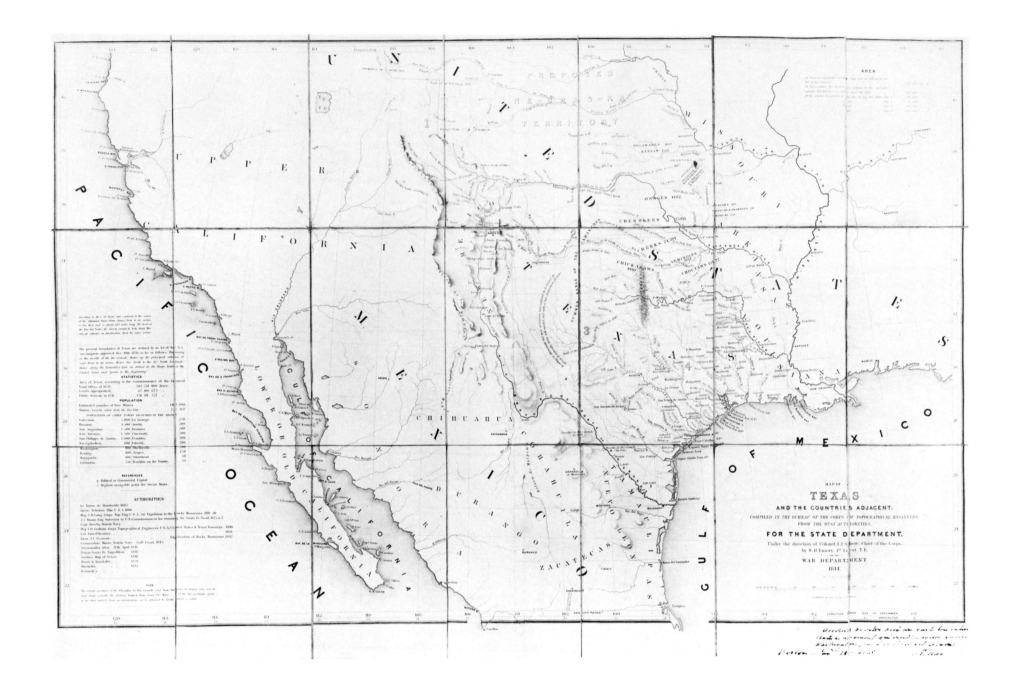

Plate 33.   William H. Emory, *Map of Texas and the Countries Adjacent ...*
(Washington, 1844).

Lithograph; 53 × 83 cm (20.9 × 32.7 in.).

In April 1844, John C. Calhoun, the American Secretary of State, and James Pinckney Henderson, the Texas minister to the United States, completed negotiations for the annexation of Texas. President John Tyler forwarded their draft treaty to the Senate for its approval, together with numerous documents concerning Texas and the annexation process. Among these documents was a *Map of Texas and the Countries Adjacent,* together with a brief memorial on the geography of the region, compiled by a young Army officer, William H. Emory. The Senate failed to ratify the treaty, and annexation became the major political issue in the presidential election of 1844. The Democratic ticket of James K. Polk and George M. Dallas ran on the slogan "The reoccupation of Oregon and the reannexation of Texas" and won by a landslide. The importance of the annexation issue, and the relevance of Emory's map to it, are revealed by Senate orders to reissue one thousand copies of the map in June and another five thousand in December.

The map itself displayed the vast territorial claims of the Republic of Texas in relation to the whole of the American Southwest. It was the first map to show correctly the full extent of the boundaries set by the Texas Congress on December 19, 1836, extending to the forty-second parallel above the sources of the Rio Grande and Arkansas River. Emory depicted the routes of numerous explorers through the region, including Pike, Stephen Long, John C. Frémont, and Josiah Gregg. The rivers in Texas and coastline were shown in clear detail, while numerous small towns in East Texas were placed and named. Little was known west of Austin although the Edwards Plateau was indicated. It is probably the best map of the region at the time of annexation.

Emory himself had never been to Texas and, consequently, he based the map not on actual observation but on information gleaned from the numerous sources available to him in the offices of the Corps of Topographical Engineers in Washington. These authorities Emory listed on the face of the map, and they included Humboldt, Pike, Long, Frémont, the United States-Texas Boundary Commission, Austin, Arrowsmith, and the General Land Office of Texas. In fashioning a synthesis from these sources, Emory was often forced to reconcile conflicting information, and it was from this process that most of his errors stemmed. In one instance, he was unable to decide the proper location of the "Presidio de Rio Grande," and therefore showed it in two places, with an explanatory note at the foot of the map. In several other cases he showed erroneous information alongside that which he had selected as true, for example in the upper courses of the Rio Grande and Arkansas.

Emory relied heavily on Arrowsmith (Plate 32) for his depiction of the Texas interior, and even repeated that map maker's egregious statement concerning the fertility, wood, and water of the Llano Estacado. Unfortunately, he did not follow Arrowsmith on the position of El Paso; instead he used the Humboldt model. His displacement of the border town to the north by half a degree, as it appeared on the Disturnell treaty map (Plate 38) three years later, was to cause Emory himself some difficulty when he served as Surveyor on the United States-Mexican Boundary Commission.

References: Streeter, *Texas* 1543; Phillips, *Maps* p. 844; Wheat 478; Day 905. Collection of Mr. and Mrs. Jenkins Garrett, Ft. Worth, Texas.

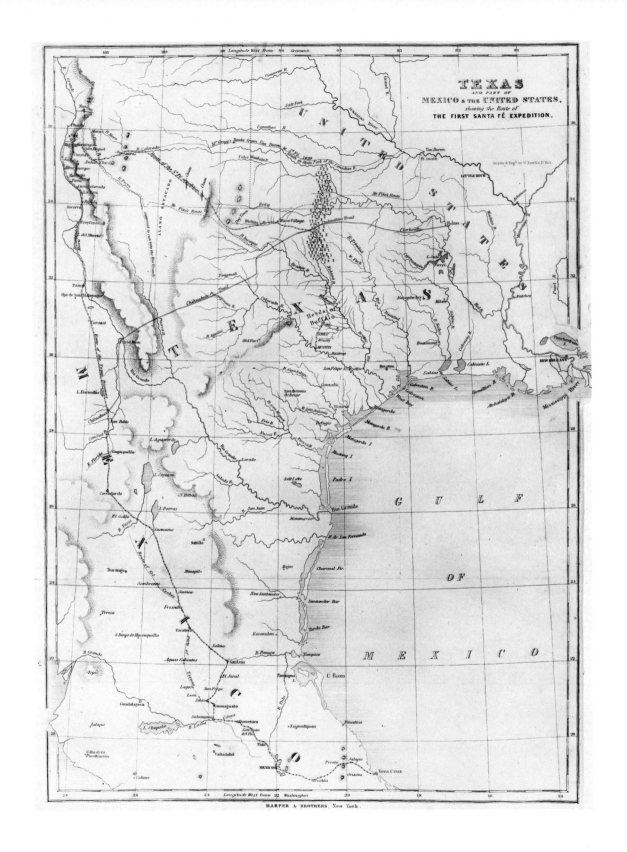

Plate 34.   W. Kemble, *Texas and Part of Mexico & the United States....*

Engraving; 40 × 29 cm (15.7 × 11.4 in.). Published in: George Wilkins Kendall, *Narrative of the Texan Santa Fe Expedition* (New York, 1844).

With independence for the Republic of Texas came the responsibility for securing its economic and political future. In 1841 President Mirabeau B. Lamar organized a sizable trade expedition to Santa Fe, the capital of New Mexico. The dual purpose was to divert to Texas some of the lucrative trade on the Santa Fe Trail and to exert military influence in the region claimed by both Texas and Mexico. Although prepared to explain peacefully the advantages to the residents of Santa Fe of citizenship in the Republic of Texas, the expedition met strong resistance and, in fact, members of the expedition were captured and marched to Mexico City as military prisoners of war.

One of the participants in this expedition was George Wilkins Kendall, a journalist who had founded the New Orleans *Picayune* in 1837. The expedition promised high adventure for the readership back home. Kendall's experiences, including imprisonment for two years in Mexico, resulted in the publication of one of the most popular books of the time, his *Narrative of the Texan Santa Fe Expedition. . . .* The book was reprinted seven times between 1844 and 1856, selling some forty thousand copies on both sides of the Atlantic. The book's distribution gave wide exposure to the map included in Kendall's narrative, done by W. Kemble and entitled *Texas and Part of Mexico and the United States, Showing the Route of the First Santa Fe Expedition.* In addition to the "Route of the Texas Prisoners," the map listed "Mr. Gregg's Route from Van Buren to Santa Fe in 1839," the "Chihuahua Trail," and "Mr. Pike's Route," which referred to an Albert Pike, not the more famous Zebulon Pike.

Although contributing little new geographical information concerning this area, the map, along with the narrative, stimulated renewed interest in Texas and represented another major step toward the inevitable solution to the Texas question later in the decade.

References: Streeter, *Texas* 1515; Wheat 483; Wagner-Camp 110.

Amon Carter Museum, Ft. Worth, Texas.

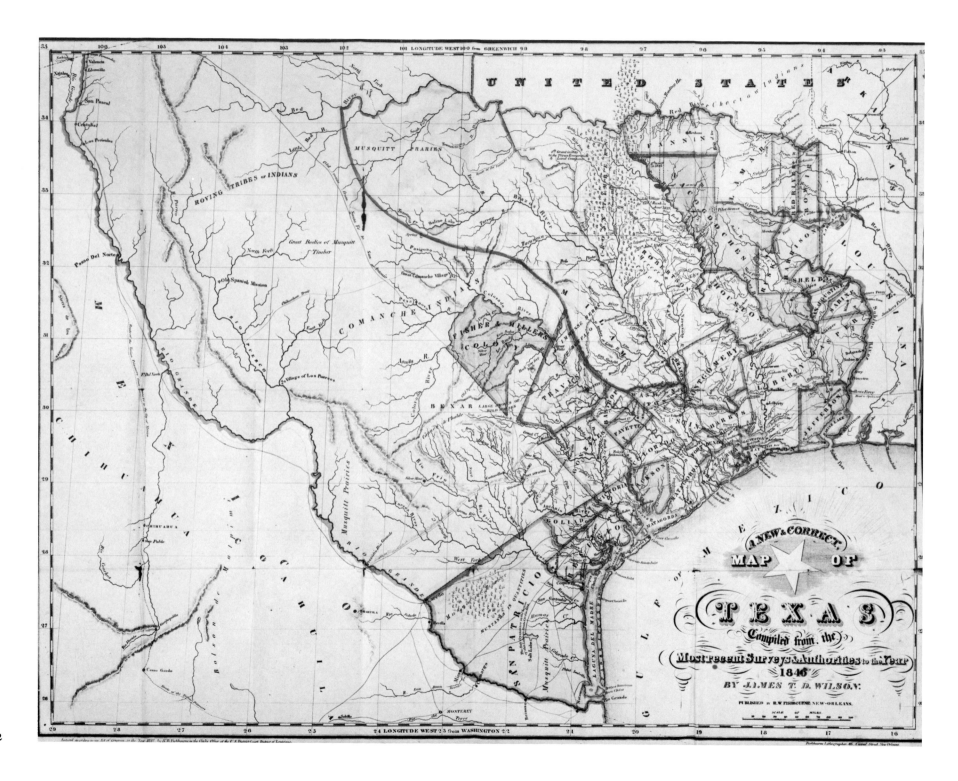

132

Plate 35.   James T. D. Wilson, *A New & Correct Map of Texas . . .* (New Orleans, 1845).

Engraving; 55 × 71 cm (21.6 × 27.9 in.).

James Wilson was only twenty-five when he made his map of Texas in 1845, but he was already a man of wide experience. Born in 1820 in St. Louis, he was abandoned by his father to be reared by friends and relatives when his mother died in 1823, and before he had reached the age of fifteen he had lived in Missouri, Mississippi, Virginia, Kentucky, and Ohio, and held an assortment of jobs. He journeyed to Texas in 1835, fought in the Texas Revolution, and eventually joined his father, by then a land speculator and sometime politician, in the real estate business in Houston. It was probably in connection with this business that Wilson made his map.

The "Authorities" on which Wilson based the map appear to be predominantly the General Land Office, which supported a guidebook and map produced in 1839, and revised in 1844 and 1845, by James Hunt and Jesse Randel. The map was extremely detailed and accurate east of the 100th meridian. The coast and the rivers of the region appeared much as they should, and other natural features such as the crosstimbers in the north and the mesquite range in the south were graphically displayed. Enchanted Rock, though unnamed, appeared as a landmark. The political features include all thirty-six counties then organized, along with their towns and settlements. He depicted several colonization ventures along with the grants to the Texas Emigration and Land Company in North Texas, and to C. Mercer. The recently established German colony in central Texas is marked as a "Dutch settlement" near the site of New Braunfels. A network of roads and trails connected the settlements throughout the area and included "Trammels Trail" in East Texas and the "Route of the Santa Fe Expedition" in the central region.

This detailed depiction of the eastern half of the Republic was in stark contrast to the dearth of information west of the 100th meridian, which gave a clear indication why many maps of the period, including Hunt and Randel's, failed to include that part. The area was for the most part blank, and the details shown were largely conjectural. The headwaters of the Colorado River were shown flowing due north from a southerly locale, then following a great bend to the east and the south. The Pecos had its headwaters below the 34th parallel, over two degrees too far south. El Paso was placed not only half a degree too far south, a common error at the time, but also was found a full degree too far east, which completely compressed the entire Transpecos region. This is of little consequence, however, since no details of that region were rendered at all. In fact, aside from the rivers and the prominently displayed "Old route from Santa Fe to San Antonio," the only information found in the western half of the State related to "roving tribes of Indians," and mythical "Great Bodies of Musquite Timber."

Wilson lived until 1902, and he twice served as the mayor of Houston, but he never made another map. His single effort is now a great rarity, surviving in only two copies, and it is perhaps the best depiction of Texas on the eve of annexation. It clearly illustrated the progress of settlement and the nearly total lack of information in the west, a region that was to remain primarily the domain of the Comanche and the coyote for another thirty years.

References: Streeter, *Texas 1627*; Phillips, *Maps* p. 844.

Everett D. Graff Collection, The Newberry Library, Chicago.

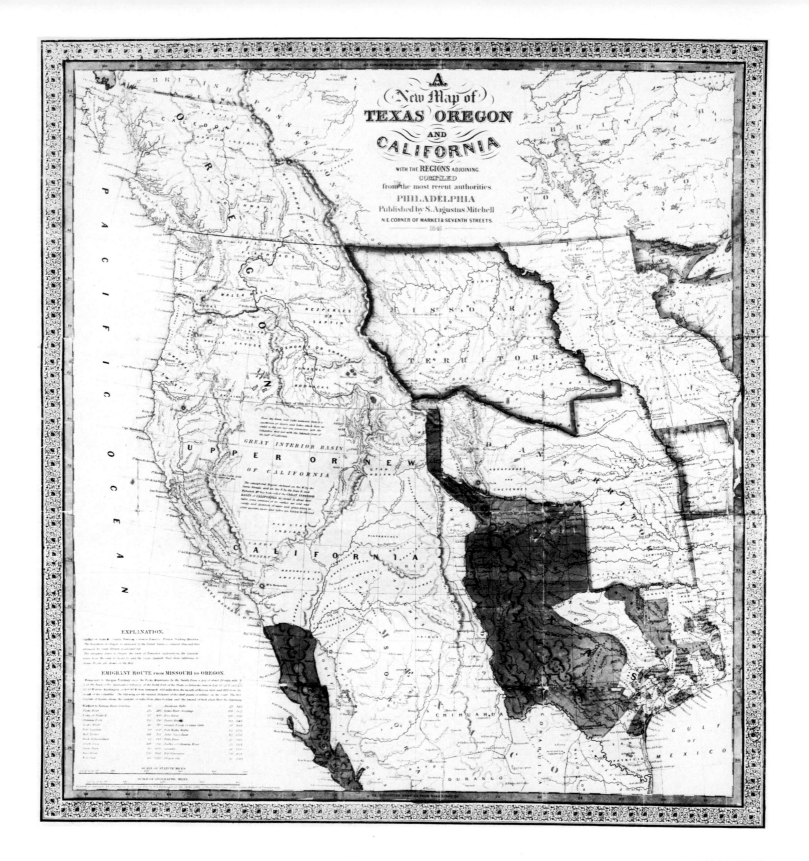

134

Plate 36.   Samuel Augustus Mitchell, *A New Map of Texas, Oregon and California . . .* (Philadelphia, 1846).

Lithograph; 51 × 47 cm (20 × 19 in.).

In the first half of the nineteenth century, international interest in the land west of the Mississippi River was both a cause and a result of new discoveries and innovations throughout the arts and sciences. Trends in the art of printing, such as the development of the lithographic process, paralleled the increased demand for up-to-date maps and charts, with the city of Philadelphia becoming one of the leading centers for the disbursement of new geographical information. The life and career of Samuel Augustus Mitchell (1792–1868) coincided with these developments, and his skills as a geographer and publisher made his name synonymous with the introduction of countless American school children to American geography.

After spending a few years of his adult life as a teacher, Mitchell became frustrated with the lack of proper teaching tools in the field of geography and decided to leave his profession in favor of a publishing career that lasted over forty years. In addition to the demands from commercial and governmental enterprises for descriptions of the latest discoveries and explorations, Mitchell's career as a publisher paralleled the development of the public school system in the United States, which provided a hungry market for his geographies.

Mitchell's ability to identify and to correlate original sources, as well as material from other map makers, was evident in his 1846 production of *A New Map of Texas, Oregon and California* with regions *adjoining. . . .* One of the first widely distributed maps showing Texas as a state in the United States, the map was published along with a forty-six page "Accompaniement," which provided the prospective traveler the latest geographical and cultural information on the territories described. Following Arrowsmith's map of Texas published in 1841 (Plate 32), Frémont's map detailing his explorations in Oregon and California, Emory's map of 1844 (Plate 33), and the work of such key western explorers as Lewis and Clark, the map showed the Texas claim to the lands of the upper Rio Grande.

The popularity of the map was no doubt heightened by the beginning of the United States's war with Mexico the same year. The concept of Manifest Destiny proved a real boon to the commercial map making industry in America, and Mitchell's extensive credits of cartographic productions during this period mirrored public interest in the important political and military decisions determining the geographical divisions of the continent. His maps were among the most popular and influential in distributing new knowledge about American expansion to a growing, eager audience.

References: Wheat 520; Day 387.

The Rosenberg Library, Galveston, Texas.

Also as Color Plate VI, p. 57.

**Plate 37. White, Gallaher, and White, *Mapa de los Estados Unidos de Méjico . . .*
(New York, 1828).**

Engraving; 74 × 105 cm (29 × 41 in.).

Plate 38. John Disturnell, *Mapa de los Estados Unidos de Méjico . . .* (New York, 1847).

Engraving; 74 × 105 cm (29 × 41 in.).

The unbridled spirit of free enterprise in the nineteenth century had a definite effect on the commercial map makers. They worked tirelessly to satisfy the demand for new information describing lands west of the Mississippi River, and in the competition to bring out material. New York City joined Philadelphia as a leading center of publishing. The career of John Disturnell (1801–77) illustrates the tremendous demand for guide books, directories, surveys, and indeed maps, which at once stimulated interest in the lands newly discovered as well as satisfied a readership eager to know more.

In 1822, perhaps the most prestigious map publisher in the United States, Henry S. Tanner, issued a new map of North America based upon the leading authorities of the day. In 1825 he reissued the southwestern portion of this map on a larger scale entitled *Map of The United States of Mexico.* In 1828, following the considerable popularity of Tanner's map, the firm of White, Gallaher, and White, located in New York, issued a copyrighted, but plagiarized, Spanish translation of Tanner's map (Plate 37).

The same plates were used in 1846 by John Disturnell to issue his own copy of the earlier map, on which he merely subsituted his name as the publisher (Plate 38). Outbreak of the United States's war with Mexico in that year resulted in Disturnell's map becoming a highly successful enterprise. It received widespread acceptance as an authority for the geography of the greater Texas region, and Disturnell issued it in twenty-three separate editions between 1846 and 1858.

Because it was the most available map of Mexico, it assumed a lasting place in history when Nicholas P. Trist, the American pleni-potentiary, used Disturnell's map in negotiating the Treaty of Guadalupe-Hidalgo, which ended the U.S.-Mexican War and extended the western boundary of the United States to the Pacific Ocean. Differences soon arose over the wording of the treaty vis-à-vis the actual depiction on Disturnell's map of the Rio Grande and the position of the city of El Paso. The lands in question were particularly important to the prospective railroad route to California and its newly discovered gold mines, a controversy which resulted in the United States purchase in 1854 of the Gadsden Territory, which rounded out the new U.S. boundaries.

Although the inaccuracies on Disturnell's map were well known by such leading explorers as Randolph B. Marcy, who called the map "one of the most inaccurate of all those I have seen . . . ," its permanent place in history was already well established. The map's spurious background, however, and its unfortunate errors, may well have contributed to government and military leaders supporting interior surveys of the American West.

References: Plate 37: Wheat 384; Day 1022; Martin, *Disturnell.* Plate 38: Wheat 540; Day 1023, 1026, 1028; Martin, *Disturnell.*

Plate 37: Eugene C. Barker Texas History Center, The University of Texas at Austin.

Plate 38: Cartographic History Library, The University of Texas at Arlington.

Also as Color Plate VII, p. 59.

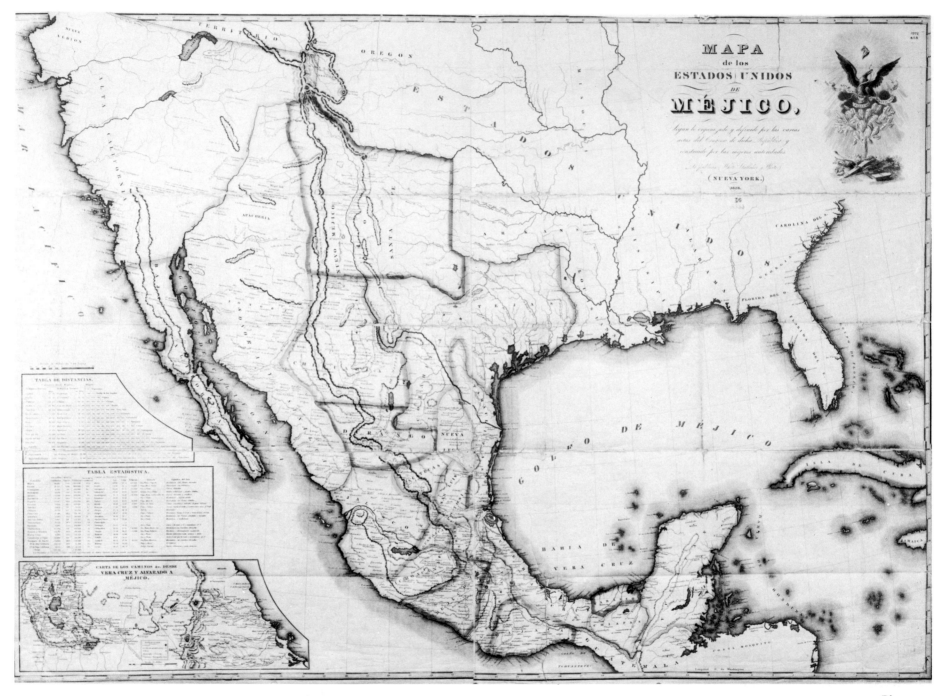

138

Plate 37.

Plate 38.

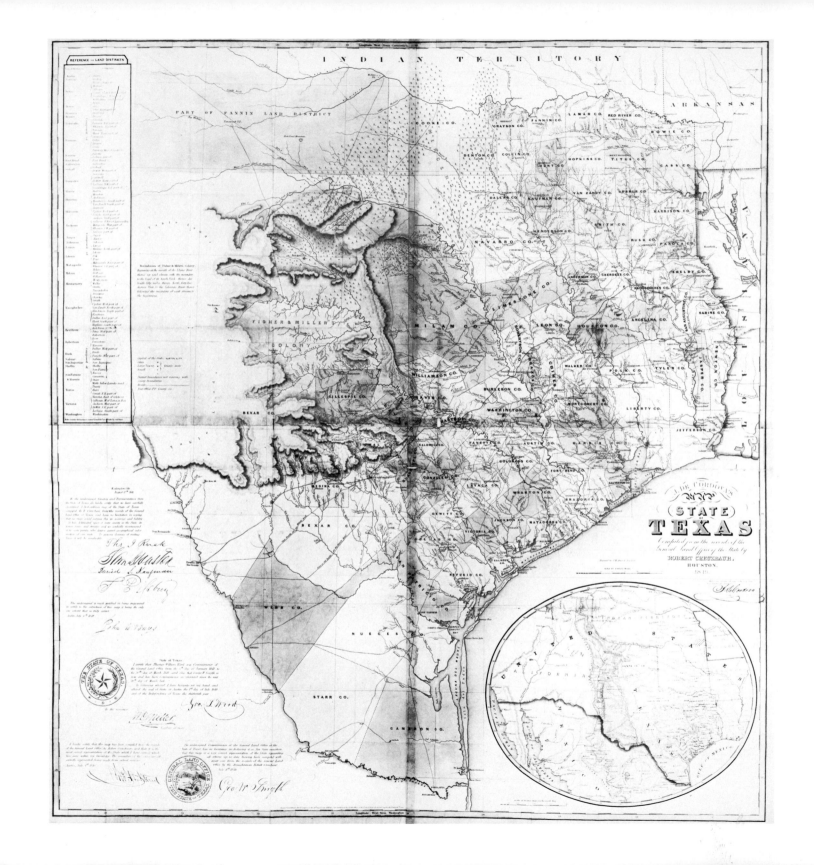

140

Plate 39. Jacob De Cordova, *J. De Cordova's Map of the State of Texas . . .* (New York, 1849).

Engraving; 93 × 89 cm (36.6 × 35 in.).

European settlement in North America repeatedly involved the question of land ownership, and resolving conflicting land claims became an integral part of the pursuit of self-determination in Texas. Spain and Mexico, to encourage the kind of settlement desired as well as to promote proper development of the land, together awarded over twenty-six million acres of land prior to the Texas Revolution. But the new Republic claimed over 250 million acres of land, leaving it poor in cash but rich in potential. After generous rewards to those who had made independence possible, Texas established awards of land for newcomers and it attempted to raise its revenues by selling land scrip in the United States. The development of these important resources prompted the Texas Congress to create a General Land Office as one of its first major acts. As the center for recordkeeping of all land transactions within the nation, this new agency naturally became the center for new cartographic productions.

One of the first talents to benefit commercially from this storehouse was Jacob de Cordova, an enthusiastic land promoter who had come to Texas from New Orleans shortly after the war for independence. Originally a native of Jamaica, de Cordova had gained experience as a printer in Philadelphia before moving to New Orleans and, after he had settled in Houston following annexation, de Cordova served a term in the state's House of Representatives. He soon moved to Austin, however, where he and his brother established the *Texas Herald.* Keenly interested in land promotion and land scrip, de Cordova employed Robert Creuzbaur, an employee of the General Land Office, to assist him in compiling a new map of Texas for publication in 1849, and their map was one of the first major cartographic productions after annexation to be based upon the records of the General Land Office. With the political geography of the state changing almost daily, the map became an important document for immigration into Texas, particularly since the recent termination of the war with Mexico had permanently secured the Texas boundary. De Cordova's map illustrated the full extent of the Texas claim by the inclusion of the inset map, which defined the Texas boundary prior to the Compromise of 1850.

De Cordova continued his promotional activities by delivering lectures on Texas throughout the United States and Europe. In 1856 he published *The Texas Immigrant and Travelers' Guide Book* and in 1858 he produced his *Texas: Her Resources and Her Public Men.*

The recordkeeping facilities of the General Land Office coupled with secure borders meant the beginning of a new chapter in the history of land in the state. Although Texas relinquished its claim to some of the lands of the upper Rio Grande in favor of a cash payment of ten million dollars, she retained ownership of all her public lands, which set her apart from most of the other states in the Union, and guaranteed a bright future for her economy.

References: Bryan and Hanak 23; Wheat 603.

The Rosenberg Library, Galveston, Texas.

Also as Frontispiece, p. ii.

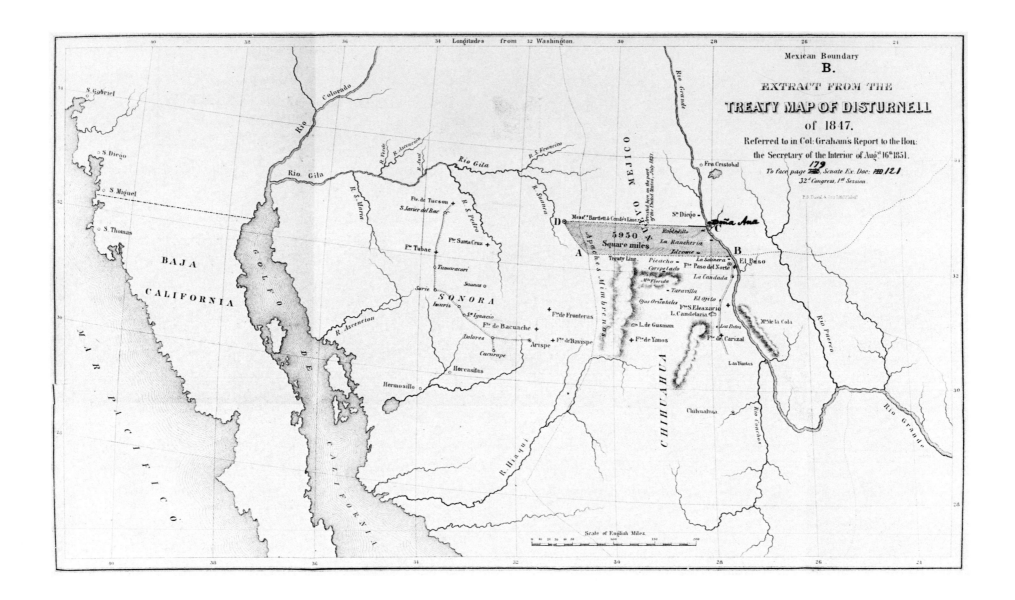

Plate 40. James D. Graham, *Mexican Boundary B. Extract from the Treaty Map of Disturnell. . . .*

Lithograph; 23 × 39 cm (9 × 15.3 in.). Published in: James D. Graham, *Report to the Hon. Secretary of the Interior . . .* (Washington, 1851).

The Treaty of Guadalupe-Hidalgo, which ended the Mexican War, specified the boundary between the United States and Mexico as running along the Rio Grande, and then "westward along the whole southern boundary of New Mexico (which runs north of the town *Paso*) to its western termination. . . ." From this point the line ran north along the western boundary of New Mexico to the Gila River, then west along that stream to its mouth on the Colorado, and then west to the Pacific below the town of San Diego. The Treaty also stipulated that the boundaries of New Mexico, which then became international border lines, should be those laid down on the Disturnell map of 1847 (Plate 38). A Joint Commission was to locate this boundary on the ground.

The history of the Mexican Boundary Survey was, perhaps more than any other episode in the American West, colored by ineptitude, personal animosity, ambition, and political interference. It was to have a significant effect on the final shape of the region.

The Commission began work in 1849 in California and, after completing the work there, adjourned to El Paso to begin locating the eastern section of the line. The American commissioner at that time, the fourth man to hold the position since the Commission was established, was John Russell Bartlett, a Rhode Island bibliophile and political appointee. He and his Mexican counterpart, General Pedro Garcia Conde, quickly determined, in attempting to locate the southern boundary of New Mexico, that the Disturnell map embodied two major errors: the Rio Grande was laid down two degrees too far west; the crucial landmark of El Paso was placed nearly forty minutes of latitude (about thirty miles) too far north. The entire region was thus distorted too far north and west with respect to the grid pattern of latitude and longitude shown on the map.

The Mexicans under Conde maintained that the boundary should be laid down with strict reference to the lines of latitude and longitude on the map, ignoring the actual positions of the Rio Grande and El Paso. The boundary thus would begin at a point about thirty miles above El Paso and continue west for about one degree of longitude before turning north to the Gila. The Americans claimed, on the other hand, that the boundary should be laid down in strict reference to the landmarks of El Paso and the Rio Grande, ignoring the latitude and longitude. The boundary would thus commence eight miles above El Paso and run west three degrees before turning north. After lengthy discussions the Commissioners compromised. Bartlett conceded that the initial point could be located thirty miles above El Paso, in the vicinity of Doña Ana, and Conde agreed that the line should run three degrees due west. A formal agreement to this so-called Bartlett-Conde Line was implemented, but the official American Surveyor, A. B. Gray, refused to sign, protesting that Bartlett had been duped. At this point Colonel James D. Graham arrived as Chief Astronomer and head of the Scientific Corps for the Army. Graham was a man of wide experience, having served as an engineer on the expedition of Stephen Long in 1819, and having commanded both the U.S.-Texas Boundary Commission and the Northwestern Boundary Commission. Graham sided with Gray against Bartlett, all three partisans submitted detailed reports to Washington, and work at surveying the boundary was halted pending a decision from the Capitol. This map is from Colonel Graham's personal copy of his printed report and contains his own manuscript notes.

The subject became a political issue of great importance in Washington. The disputed territory not only included rich copper mines and other mineral deposits, but it also contained what was agreed upon as the only practical route for a southern railroad to California. Naturally the Mexicans could not be expected to back down from a favorable agreement entered into in good faith, but neither could the U.S. government afford to relinquish nearly six thousand square miles of territory that had been won on the battlefield and at the conference table. The issue was defused in 1853 with the Gadsden Purchase, a treaty in which the United States obtained the disputed territory, as well as additional lands and other Mexican concessions, in return for a cash payment. The entire episode proved to the public and to Government the value of accurate maps and efficient surveys.

Reference: Wheat 718.

Jenkins Garrett Library, The University of Texas at Arlington.

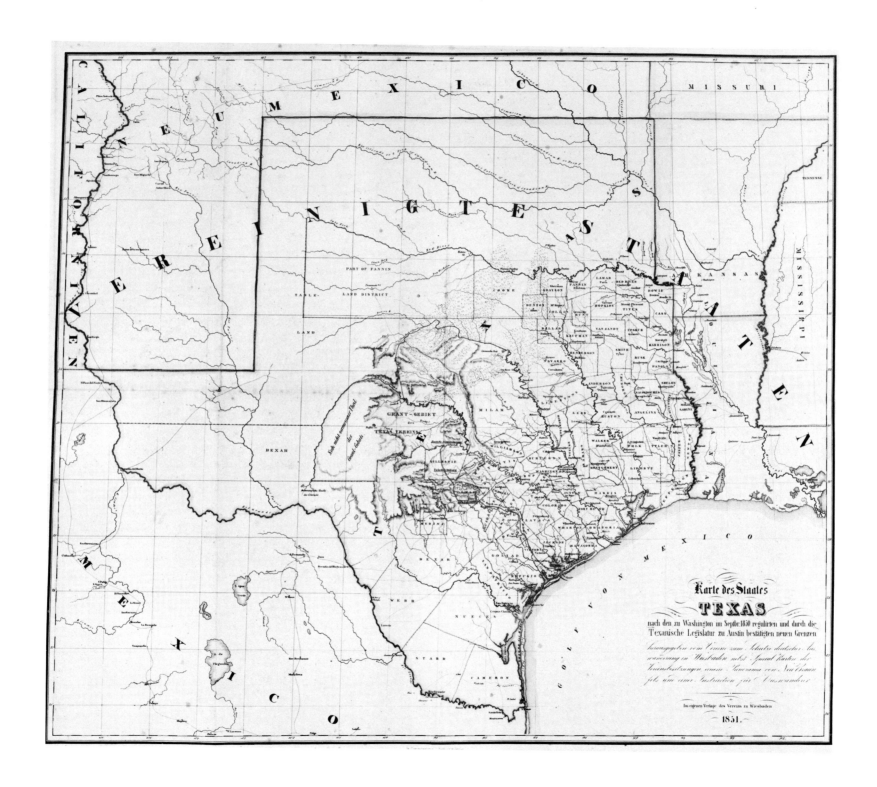

Karte des Staates

TEXAS

nach den zu Washington im Septbr 1850 regulirten und durch die
Texanische Legislatur zu Austin bestätigten neuen Grenzen

herausgegeben vom Verein zum Schutze deutscher Auswanderung zu Wiesbaden nebst Special Karten der Vereinsbesitzungen einem Panorama von Neu-Braunfels und einer Instruction für Auswanderer

Im eigenen Verlage des Vereins zu Wiesbaden

1851.

144

Plate 41. Verein zum Schütze Deutscher Einwanderer in Texas, *Karte des Staates Texas . . .* (Wiesbaden, 1851).

Lithograph; 58 × 66 cm (22.8 × 26 in.).

In the fifteen years between annexation and the Civil War, immigrants streamed into Texas from the socially and politically torn German states of central and western Europe. Many of these settlers came to Texas under the auspices of the Society for the Protection of German Emigrants in Texas (Verein zum Schütze Deutscher Einwanderer in Texas, often known as the Adelsverein). Originally formed in 1842 by a group of German nobles "for the purpose of purchasing land in the free state of Texas," the Verein expanded its aims in 1844 to include financing and assisting German emigrants, and their agent in Texas, Prince Carl von Solms-Braunfels, purchased the rights to a grant originally made in 1842 to Henry F. Fisher and Burchard Miller. The settlement of New Braunfels was founded in 1845 as a way-station for settlers en route to the Fisher-Miller Grant, and by 1847 the Verein had established nearly 8,000 immigrants in the grant. Financial restraints forced the group to reduce its active operations in that year, but it continued for a number of years to offer advice and information to emigrants from the German regions of Europe to Texas.

In 1851 the Verein published a folder of *Instructions*, which included a catechism of advice for prospective emigrants, a report of the society's activities to that point, maps and views of the towns of Fredricksburg, New Braunfels, and Indianola, and a general map of the state. The rapid progress of westward settlement is evident in this *Karte des Staates Texas:* eighty counties are delineated along with numerous towns and settlements and the roads connecting them. The title of the map called attention to the Compromise of 1850 boundary in the northwest, which was "adjusted in Washington in September of 1850 and confirmed by the Texas Legislature in Austin." In this respect the town of El Paso was almost properly located, and the boundary proceeded from that point quite correctly until it reached the 100th meridian, where, instead of turning due south to intersect the Red River,

it curiously continued east to the Arkansas line, and thus assigned most of present Oklahoma to Texas. Like most maps of the period, the portion of the State west of the 100th meridian was left almost blank, but the Pecos River was shown with remarkable accuracy and its source was properly located just east of Santa Fe.

The purpose of the map was to show the location of the Verein's grant, and prominently displayed among the hachures representing the Edwards Plateau, was the "Grant District of the Texas Society" ("Grant-Gebiet des Texas Vereins"). The route from the port of Indianola to the German settlements ("Deutsche Niederlassungen") was highlighted, and the western portion of the grant was shown as not yet surveyed ("Noch nicht vermessener Theil"). The original grant to Fisher and Miller stipulated a boundary running up the Llano River from its mouth to the source of its northern branch, then due south for fifty miles, then west to the Colorado River, and then down that river to the place of beginning. The Colorado River was shown on this map with its "supposed source" ("Muthmassliche Quelle") far to the south, near the Rio Grande. Since the river's source was actually to the northwest, not far from present Lubbock, the southern boundary stipulated by the grant never intersected it. Later the problem was recognized and the boundaries of the grant were adjusted so that the line ran northwest instead of west, but it still failed to find the Colorado. Consequently, a gap existed in the western boundary of the grant until the contract lapsed. This demonstrated a common difficulty, for both the grantee and the government, in assigning and locating grants when the topography of the region was still imperfectly known.

Reference: Day 1997.

Cartographic History Library, The University of Texas at Arlington.

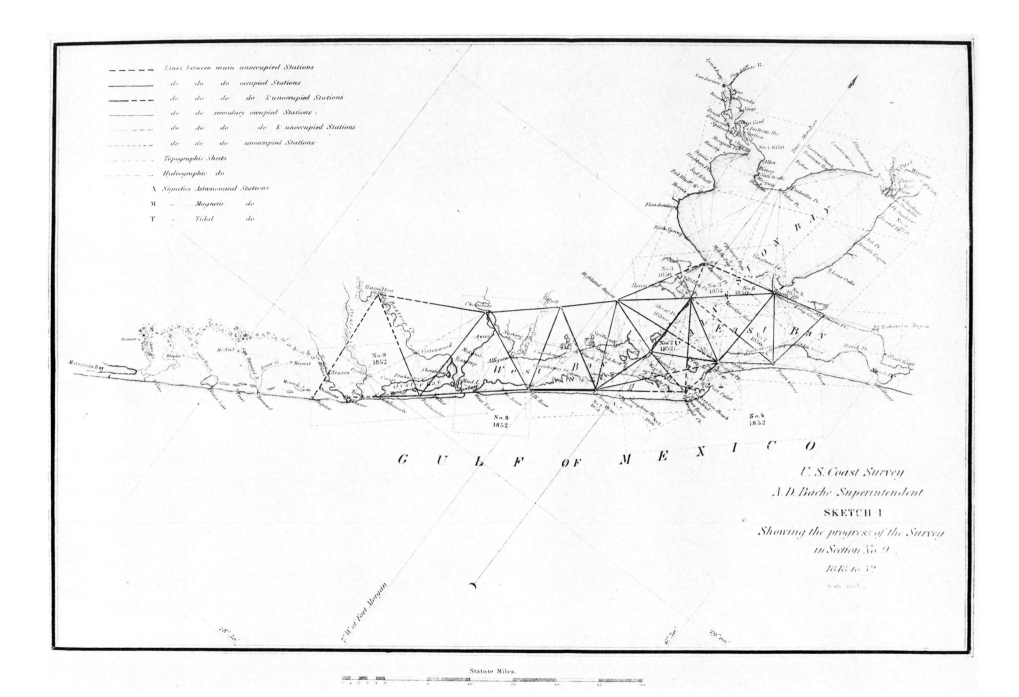

Lines between main unoccupied Stations
do   do   do   occupied Stations
do   do   do   do & unoccupied Stations
do   do   secondary occupied Stations
do   do   do   do & unoccupied Stations
do   do   do   unoccupied Stations
Topographic Sheets
Hydrographic   do
A   Signifies Astronomical Stations
M   "   Magnetic   do
T   "   Tidal   do

GULF OF MEXICO

U.S. Coast Survey
A.D. Bache Superintendent
SKETCH I
Showing the progress of the Survey
in Section No 9.
1848 to 52

Statute Miles.

Plate 42. United States Coast Survey, *Sketch I Showing the Progress of the Survey in Section No. 9....*

Engraving; 19×54 cm (7.5×21 in.). Published in: *Report of the Superintendent of the Coast Survey Showing the Progress of the Survey in 1852* (Washington, 1853).

On February 10, 1807 President Thomas Jefferson signed a bill creating the United States Coast Survey. The new agency was responsible for conducting detailed surveys of the young nation's coastal areas and producing charts based on this work. Its creation followed realization of the urgent need to ensure the safety of mariners, ships, and cargoes by supplying information about the shoals, reefs, and navigational hazards among which they moved while carrying the nation's commerce. Because of this concern for maritime trade, the Survey was established under Albert Gallatin, Secretary of Commerce, who in turn selected a young Swiss engineer, Ferdinand Hassler, then employed as a mathematics teacher at West Point, to head the new agency. This selection was to have a profound effect on the course of the Survey's work.

Hassler was a perfectionist who envisioned the division of the Survey's work into three branches—geodetic, hydrographic, and topographic, of which the geodetic was most important. Geodesy is the science concerned with the measurement and description of the size and shape of the earth, and includes large scale surveys for determining positions and elevations of points for which the size and shape of the earth must be taken into account. The original conception of the Survey was much less ambitious and did not include geodetic work, but Hassler rightly saw that the Survey's work would prove truly useful and stand the test of time only if its detailed triangulation could be attached to a firm framework of geodetically determined points. This insistence caused lengthy delays in the work of the Survey and endless political problems with a Congress bent on more immediate, less precise results, but it ultimately was the basis for the extremely accurate maps and charts the Survey produced.

By the time of Hassler's death in 1843 the foundation for the survey of the coast had been laid and the detailed surveys of the ports and harbors were begun at New York. Hassler was succeeded by Alexander Dallas Bache, a great-grandson of Benjamin Franklin and grandson of Alexander Dallas, Madison's Secretary of the Treasury. Bache's academic and intellectual credentials were impeccable, and he followed Hassler's plan faithfully, adapting it to fit the needs of the expanding United States. The addition of Texas, California, Oregon, and Washington to the nation at the close of the Mexican War nearly doubled the length of coastline under the Survey's charge, and Bache pursued the extended surveying and charting operations with vigor and scientific rigor.

Bache divided the work of the Survey into eleven sections, of which the Texas coast was section nine. Work began in this area in 1848 and by 1852 the annual reports of the Survey included detailed sketches displaying the progress of operations. Beginning from a base line along the Gulf on Galveston Island, triangulations were run in virtually every direction and key points were determined from the easternmost reaches of Galveston Bay to the mouth of the Brazos. The same annual report also included a detailed sketch of Galveston Bay, with the soundings of all the approaches and with navigational directions included.

The work of the Coast Survey not only resulted in the most accurate charts possible of the coastal waters of the nation, ensuring the safety and the reliability of maritime traffic, it also pioneered the modern techniques and equipment utilized by later surveys in the interior. Moreover, it provided the precise geodetic framework on which these later surveys were based. The work of the U.S. Geological Survey, the various state surveys, and even the surveys of the Army's Topographical Corps were thus to some extent grounded in the work of the Coast Survey. Even more important, the early creation of the Coast Survey embodied a recognition on the part of the federal government of a new responsibility, that of developing and disseminating maps and charts to promote the safety and welfare of the people. It is thus in the political as well as technical and scientific groundwork of the Coast Survey that the later progress of other government surveyors is founded. Thus, in more ways than one, the country became known from the coastline inward.

Sid Richardson Collection, Cartographic History Library, The University of Texas at Arlington.

Plate 43. Joseph Hutchins Colton, *Colton's Map of the United States of America, the British Provinces, Mexico and the West Indies . . .* (New York, 1854).

Engraving; 130 × 145 cm (51 × 57 in.).

The Compromise of 1850 fixed the geographical shape of Texas in the United States. Its settlement, though, continued for some time. Although the early settlers in Texas were predominantly from the South, steady immigration and a diverse economy meant that Texas had much in common with the other emerging states and territories in the new American West. The discovery of gold in California, which coincided with the peace treaty with Mexico, lured explorers, settlers, scientists, and the military farther west; the prospects for a transcontinental railroad further encouraged the traffic west. All of this interest in going west opened up new markets and new demands in the cartographic centers of the East.

In New York, the firm of J. H. Colton emerged as a leading supplier for these demands. He published a major, enlarged map of the United States, showing most of the continent, reissued it in 1853 incorporating new information on the American West, and issued it again in 1854. Although it does not depict the boundary changes resulting from the Gadsden Purchase, the map was up-to-date in most of its information and was one of the most influential of that period. Colton's rendering and details in Texas were based largely on those of de Cordova's map of Texas.

The vignettes on the map provide an interesting visual compliment to the information disseminated in the document itself, adding a distinctive American flavor to the nineteenth century map trade.

Reference: Wheat 747, 799.

Sid Richardson Collection, Cartographic History Library, The University of Texas at Arlington.

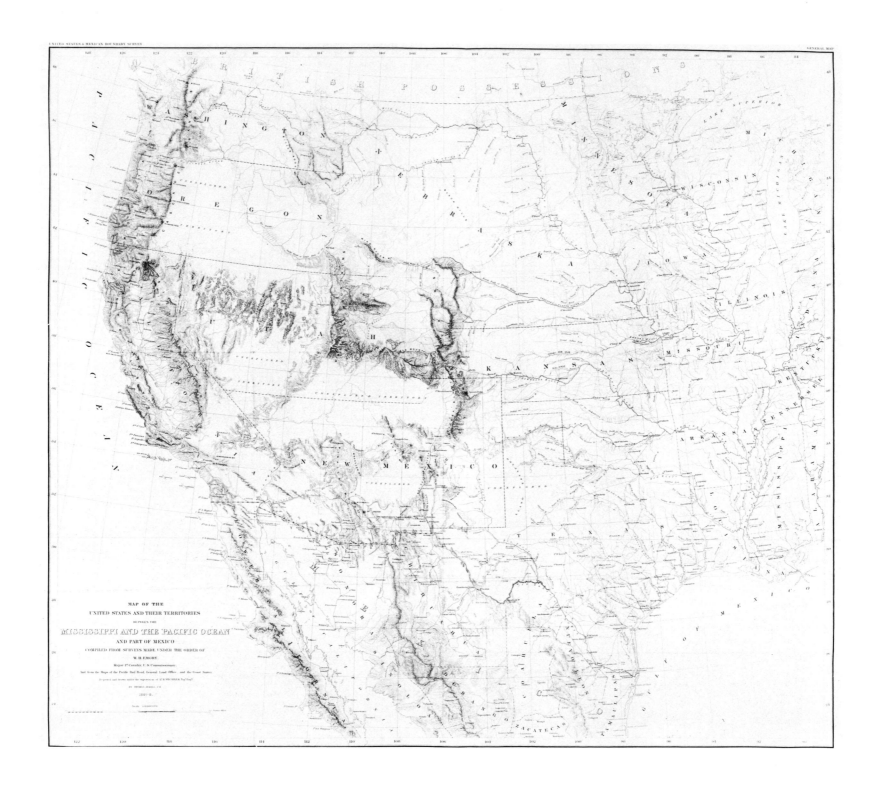

MAP OF THE
UNITED STATES AND THEIR TERRITORIES
BETWEEN THE
MISSISSIPPI AND THE PACIFIC OCEAN
AND PART OF MEXICO
COMPILED FROM SURVEYS MADE UNDER THE ORDER OF
W. H. EMORY,
Major 1st Cavalry, U. S. Commissioner;
And from the Maps of the Pacific Rail Road, General Land Office, and the Coast Survey.

Plate 44.   William H. Emory, *Map of the United States and Their Territories Between the Mississippi and the Pacific Ocean and Part of Mexico. . . .*

Engraving; 87 × 50 cm (34 × 19.5 in.). Published in: *Report of the United States and Mexican Boundary Survey . . .* (Washington, 1851).

William H. Emory first joined the Mexican Boundary Survey in 1849 as Chief Astronomer and Commander of the Military Escort. He was to assist the Commissioner and the Surveyor in their work and to provide protection from the Indians; however, he and the men in his command actually performed much of the Survey's work. He served under difficult physical and political circumstances and was actually for a brief time named Acting Commissioner during one of the numerous political squabbles that marred the work of the Survey. He returned to Washington in 1850 to complete the official survey maps for the San Diego-Gila River section of the line. When controversy over the Bartlett-Conde compromise line arose in New Mexico in 1851, Emory was again detailed to the field, first in the role of Chief Astronomer, then with the added title of Surveyor. While the work in surveying the line west from El Paso was suspended pending a settlement over the diplomatic problem in Washington, Emory and his men busied themselves surveying the course of the Rio Grande from New Mexico to the Gulf. In this work the great river was actually explored for the first time, and much of the Transpecos and Big Bend regions of Texas were surveyed. By September 1853, the river survey was virtually completed and, with still no settlement of the New Mexico boundary dispute, Emory returned to Washington again to complete the maps. Less than a year later, in August 1854, Emory was named Commissioner and Chief Astronomer for the new Commission to survey the boundary of the Gadsden Purchase, which had finally settled the old New Mexico controversy. Pre-

siding over the entire work, Emory demonstrated the way a boundary survey could operate when efficiently organized by experienced personnel and unhindered by political appointees. The work was quickly completed and Emory was back in Washington by October 1855.

After completing these assignments, Emory compiled and published a monumental report of the entire work of the boundary survey. This report was not only a political and geographic landmark, but it was also an important scientific contribution in its documentation of the flora and fauna of the American Southwest. It contained a large map of the entire country west of the Mississippi River, and comparison of it with Emory's map published in 1844 (Plate 33) shows dramatically the vast amount of information gathered concerning the region in the short time since it had been acquired by the Treaty of Guadalupe-Hidalgo. The map depicted the work of the boundary survey and the important explorations of the entire West under numerous government agencies and bureaus. In spite of the marvelous detail, though, Emory was not afraid to admit ignorance of some areas, such as the Llano Estacado, which were left blank and labeled "unexplored." Emory's map documented the West as it was actually known, but also revealed what remained to be explored.

Reference: Wheat 822.

Amon Carter Museum, Ft. Worth, Texas.

PLATE LIV

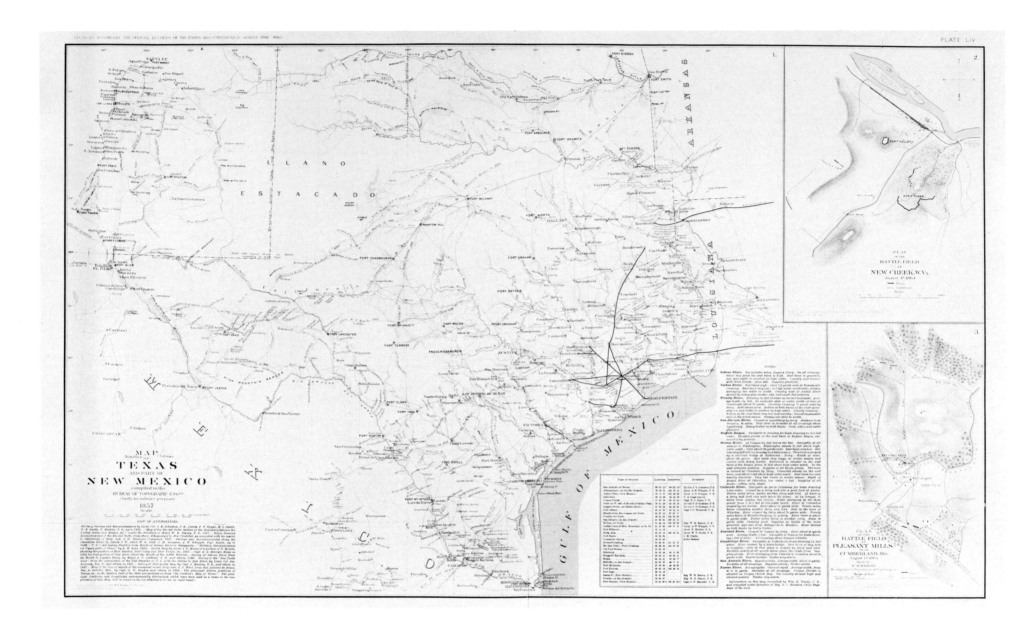

Plate 45. United States, Army Corps of Engineers, *Map of Texas and Part of New Mexico. . . .*

Lithograph; 42 × 69 cm (16.5 × 27.1 in.). Published in: *Atlas to Accompany the Official Records of the Union and Confederate Armies . . .* (Washington, 1880).

With the onset of the Civil War, the federal exploration and mapping efforts in the West ceased, and many of the federal troops there either withdrew or surrendered. In Texas, after the capitulation of the troops in San Antonio under General Twiggs, the war lapsed for nearly a year. But in December 1862, Nathaniel P. Banks, a politically appointed general from Massachusetts, was named to command the Union Department of the Gulf, and operations in the Texas region commenced shortly thereafter. Banks presided over an unsuccessful attack on Galveston, and troops under his command were decisively defeated by an inferior force at the Battle of Sabine Pass in 1863. A more successful effort under Banks's command managed to hold the lower Rio Grande for a time, but the federal troops were eventually evacuated in August 1864. The final Union attempt at a Texas invasion under Banks led to the ill-fated Red River Campaign, in which the federals were defeated at the Battle of Mansfield and forced once again to retire.

Shortly after assuming command of the Gulf in 1862 and while planning his offensives in New Orleans, Banks dispatched a report to Washington containing a map of the Texas region. The map had been prepared from various sources shortly before the war, and it was an excellent example of a military planning document. Presented as notes were descriptions of the tactical features of an area where operations were contemplated. The sources were listed on its face, and these included the numerous reports of military expeditions and operations in Texas and the surrounding countries from the Mexican War through the late 1850s, as well as the works of the Boundary Survey and the General Land Office. The focus of the map was clearly on military considerations—avenues of communication and possible routes for troop movement. Roads across the territory were shown in great detail, ac-

companied by notes on the availability of wood and water, supplies, and stream crossings, as well as the nature of the topography and the passability of the terrain. The overland mail route from Fort Smith in Arkansas to El Paso and beyond was prominently displayed as the major east-west artery through the region. An extensive set of notes in the lower right described the major rivers as both avenues of, and hindrances to, communication, noting their navigability and the various bridges and fords. The map also dramatically highlighted the network of railroads around Houston and in the vicinity of Victoria and Marshall, lines that were extremely important for transporting troops and therefore likely routes of invasion.

The numerous military details shown in Texas, New Mexico, and the Indian Territory revealed the heritage of Indian wars: troops had been stationed in the region during the decade prior to the Civil War. The edge of the western frontier in Texas was clearly shown paralleling the route of the overland mail route, proceeding through forts Lancaster, Chadbourne, Phantom Hill, and Belknap. West of this line was the range of the Comanche and Kiowa. The Rio Grande Valley in New Mexico showed a populated area protected by a string of forts, to the east of which was a similar blank area, crossed only by Indian trails.

Though drawn originally in 1857 and utilized by Banks in 1862, the map was not published until the 1880s, when it appeared in the *Atlas to Accompany the Official Records of the Union and Confederate Armies.* It has served to document the status of the frontier in the Southwest immediately prior to the great American conflict, and to illustrate some of the operations in that war.

Cartographic History Library, The University of Texas at Arlington.

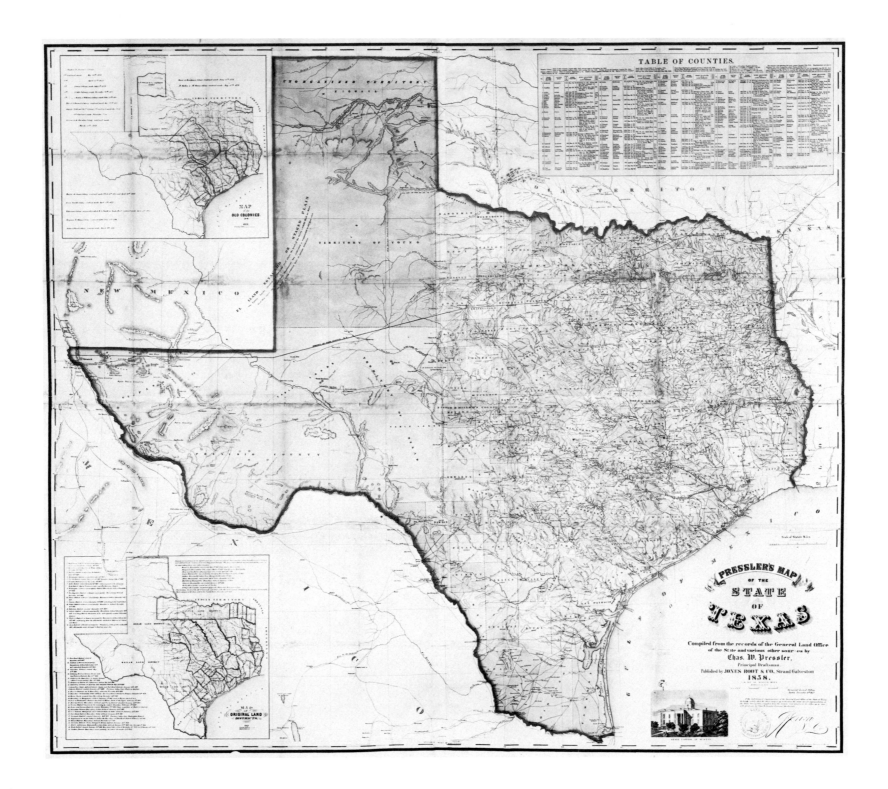

PRESSLER'S MAP
OF THE
STATE
OF
TEXAS

Compiled from the records of the General Land Office
of the State and various other sources by
Chas. W. Pressler,
Principal Draftsman.
Published by JONES ROOT & CO, Strand Galveston
1858.

TABLE OF COUNTIES.

MAP
of the
OLD COLONIES

MAP
of the
ORIGINAL LAND
DISTRICTS.

Plate 46. Charles W. Pressler, *Pressler's Map of the State of Texas . . .* (Galveston, 1858).

Lithograph; 120 × 130 cm (47.2 × 51 in.).

The role of the General Land Office in mapping Texas in the second half of the nineteenth century centered in the career of Charles William Pressler, who immigrated to Texas from Prussia in 1846. As a trained surveyor, Pressler moved from Galveston to Austin, where he was employed by the noted map maker, Jacob de Cordova, to conduct surveying expeditions for the benefit of de Cordova's cartographic productions. In 1850, Pressler joined the staff of the General Land Office, where he collected and disseminated information concerning the geography of Texas until his retirement in 1899. Having come to Texas as part of the Adelsverein, an organization created for the purpose of bringing German immigrants into Texas (see Plate 41), Pressler was keenly aware of the needs of potential immigrants. He aided these people by making available travel literature and maps of the period.

After de Cordova employed Pressler to assist in correcting and revising his map of Texas, which was first published in 1849 (Plate 39), de Cordova sold his rights to J. H. Colton in 1855, at which time Pressler began work on a map of Texas on his own. In 1858 Pressler published a magnificent new map of Texas, one of the truly outstanding large scale maps of the state of Texas produced in the nineteenth century. Pressler produced new editions of this map in 1862 and again in 1867, at which time he entitled the map *Travellers' Map of the State of Texas*. That the map was printed in Galveston provided an interesting statement on the development of the arts and sciences in Texas in the nineteenth century.

The accuracy of Pressler's map was a major improvement in presenting Texas geography, particularly in the western areas of the state where errors and guesswork had been common. Pressler emphasized the emerging political entities within the state, as well as accurately depicting the rivers, streams, and developing road system within the state.

In addition to his work at the General Land Office, Pressler served as a captain in the Confederacy, working with the engineering department, and he later worked for the United States government in various surveys, including an inspection of a number of military forts in West Texas. But his map of 1858 continued as one of his most important contributions, providing a remarkably accurate picture of Texas during a period when the growth of knowledge about the state's geography matched its growth in population. This map was the best description of Texas on the eve of yet another in the series of political changes in the nineteenth century—the lowering of the Stars and Stripes and the raising of the Stars and Bars.

References: Phillips, *Maps* p. 845; Bryan and Hanak p. 12; Day 1201.

Courtesy of Mr. Herman Pressler, Houston, Texas.

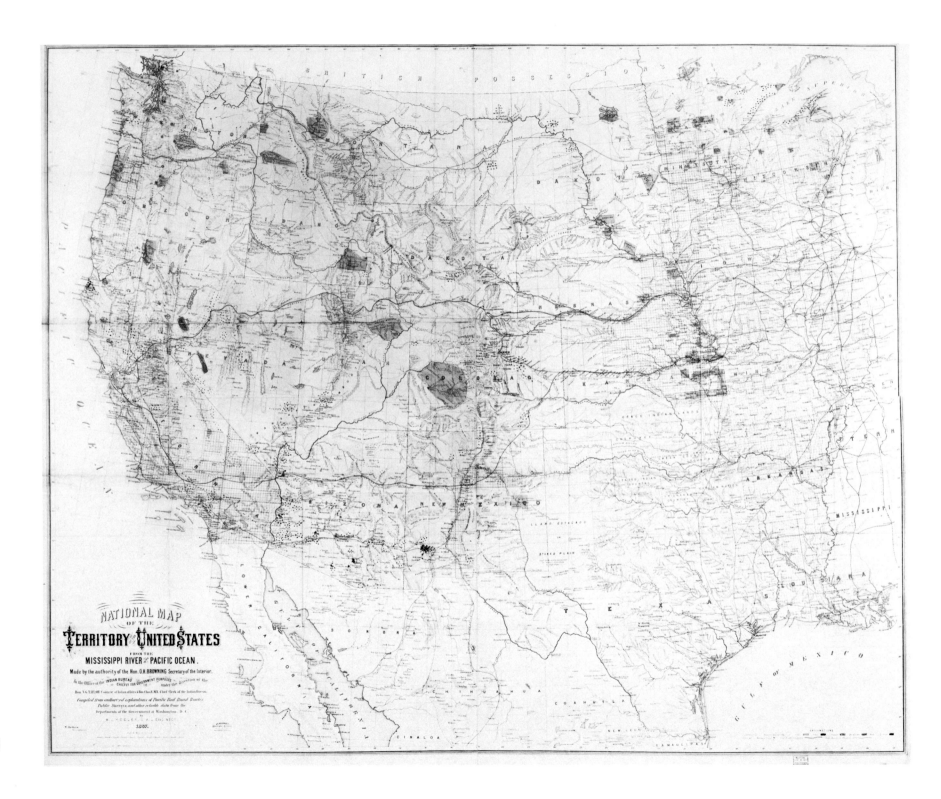

NATIONAL MAP
OF THE
TERRITORY UNITED STATES
FROM THE
MISSISSIPPI RIVER AND PACIFIC OCEAN.

Made by the authority of the Hon. O.H. BROWNING Secretary of the Interior.

Plate 47. William J. Keeler, *National Map of the Territory of the United States from the Mississippi to the Pacific Ocean . . .* (Washington, 1867).

Lithograph; 120 × 146 cm (47.2 × 57.5 in.).

The development of rail transportation was one of the most important technological innovations of the nineteenth century. It occasioned a revolution in communication, linking independent farmers and manufacturers to national—even worldwide—markets, and expanding personal horizons by bringing once-distant places within reach. But support for the railroad and its eventual construction came in fits and starts. When gold was discovered in the new U.S. territory of California in 1848, the rail lines scarcely stretched west of the Mississippi. The difficulties in transportation and communication evident in the gold rush emphasized the tenuous nature of the link between the east and west coasts of the continent. The public at large, led by the vested interests of the rail companies, pressured Congress into funding numerous explorations to determine the most practical route to the Pacific. Led by the Army, the Pacific railroad surveys penetrated for the first time much of the new territory won by the United States in the Mexican War; these expeditions became known as the Great Reconnaissance. The report of these surveys, concluded in 1855, was published in twelve massive volumes and included documentation of all the botanical, zoological, geological, and geographical discoveries. A large map compiled by Lt. G. K. Warren was included in the report. It displayed all of the information gleaned from the great discoveries, as well as the four practical railroad routes to the Pacific.

The Civil War interrupted interest in western railroad construction, but not long after the cessation of hostilities the various rail companies began to compete with each other for government subsidies and private investors. In 1867, seeking to take advantage of public interest in all aspects of the West, but particularly the railroad routes, William J. Keeler, an engineer working in the Indian Bureau, published a large, attractive map of the entire country west of the Mississippi. In spite of its official sounding title, the map was privately printed and copyrighted by Keeler personally, and was consequently a trade item, not a government document. The map displayed the country in remarkable detail and, while it was largely based on Warren's map as well

as the Pacific railroad surveys, it was no mere copy. The Keeler map highlighted the railroad routes, particularly those of the Union Pacific and the Northern Pacific. Numerous towns and settlements were shown for the first time on a general map. As a product no doubt of Keeler's own employment with the Indian Bureau, the various Indian reservations were clearly shown and identified by a color scheme, an early use of this thematic device. While the map was full of factual information, it also projected many hopeful portrayals of the progress of the railroads, and a few outright distortions as well. For example, Keeler claimed that the Colorado River of the West is shown "from actual survey," when in fact no such surveys had been completed in 1867, and consequently no hint was given of that river's Grand Canyon.

The map was accompanied by a short set of "Notes" in which Keeler discussed the origins of the map and pointed out its advantages. After claiming that his was the only one published showing all of the Pacific Railroad routes, Keeler made a marvelous, if ingenuous, summation of one important aspect of Manifest Destiny and the driving force behind the whole westward movement:

> The location of all the known mines of gold, silver, copper, and other valuable metals, are carefully and accurately noted. . . . Of the ultimate value of these widely extended depositories of the precious metals no estimate can be made; but that they are destined to exert a mighty influence upon our country and upon the entire world, as indeed they have already done, is beyond question. It is the attraction of these hidden treasures, more than anything else, that is drawing those great lines of railroad across the Continent. . . .

Reference: Wheat 1170.

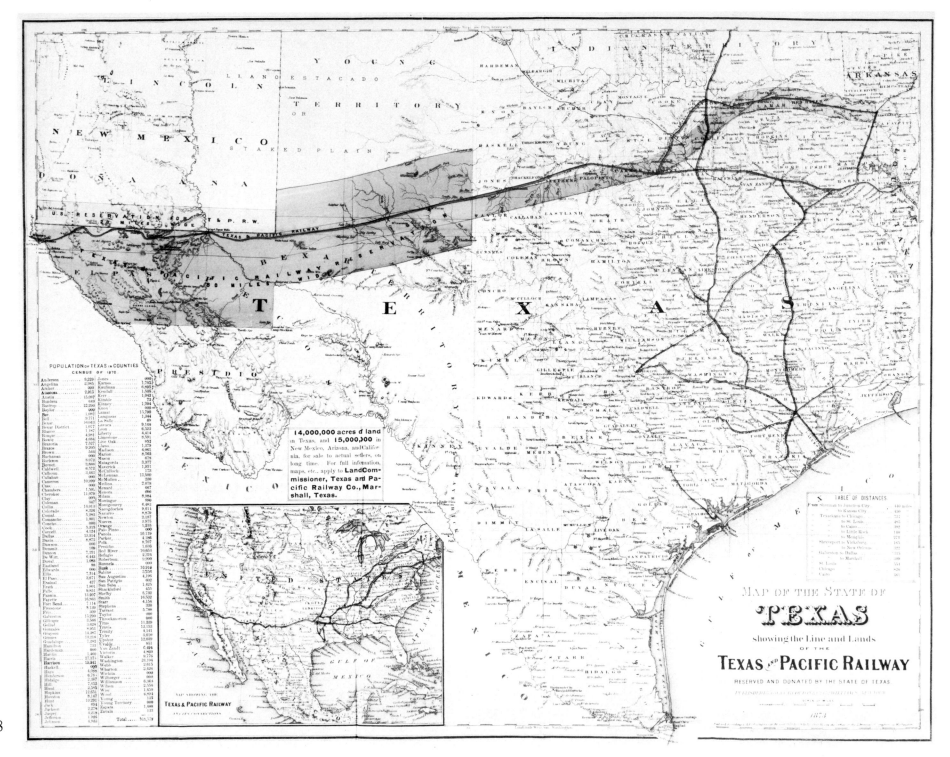

Plate 48.   George Woolworth Colton, *Map of the State of Texas Showing the Line and Lands of the Texas and Pacific Railway. . . .*

Engraving; 47 × 60 cm (18.5 × 23.6 in.). Published in: *Notes on the Texas and Pacific Railway . . .*
(Philadelphia, 1873).

The Texas and Pacific Railroad was perhaps the greatest of the early railroads in Texas. It was chartered by the federal government on March 3, 1871, and authorized to construct a line from Marshall, Texas, to San Diego, California. For this work it was granted a subsidy by the United States government of twenty sections of public land per mile of track laid in California, and forty sections per mile in New Mexico and Arizona. The state of Texas, which had retained ownership of its public lands at the time of annexation, granted the railroad twenty sections per mile of track laid in Texas. Work on the line was actually begun in 1873, laying track west from Marshall under the indefatigable engineer, Grenville M. Dodge. The line had reached Fort Worth by 1876. In 1880 the "T and P" was purchased by the great railroad magnate Jay Gould, who pushed the line westward, finally connecting with the Southern Pacific line at Sierra Blanca, ninety-two miles east of El Paso, in 1881.

From 1873 to 1881 the Texas and Pacific constructed 972 miles of track in Texas, entitling it to over 12.4 million acres of public land. Since, however, all of the track laid west of Fort Worth was completed after the time specified in the charter, the railroad actually only received a total of 5.1 million acres.

When construction began in 1873, the railroad issued a series of promotional pamphlets, extolling the assets and advantages of the Texas and Pacific over rival companies. Most of these contained maps of one type or another, demonstrating the proposed route and its beneficial connections to the east and the west. The map published in *Notes on the Texas and Pacific Railway,* however, was different from these. Based on a standard map of the state published by G. W. Colton, son and successor to J. H. Colton, the map displayed not only the proposed route and the area which it serviced, but also highlighted in red the region in which the company proposed to locate the vast land subsidies provided by the state. The line cut a wide swath across the entire state, and this graphic depiction of the prominence of the T and P must surely have proved to be an impressive and persuasive argument for potential investors.

Railroad construction in Texas in the 1870s outstripped all other construction in the entire country. It contributed substantially to pushing the frontier farther west by improving communication through and within the state. It also provided an economic boom to the region, markedly benefiting such associated businesses as the East Texas lumber industry, which was called upon to furnish the raw materials for ties, trestles, cattle pens, and shipping facilities. In this way the industrialization of the state began. In addition, the alienation of public land, so graphically depicted by this map, also contributed substantially to the end of the frontier and to the accurate mapping of the region.

Cartographic History Library, The University of Texas at Arlington.

Also as Color Plate VIII, p. 61.

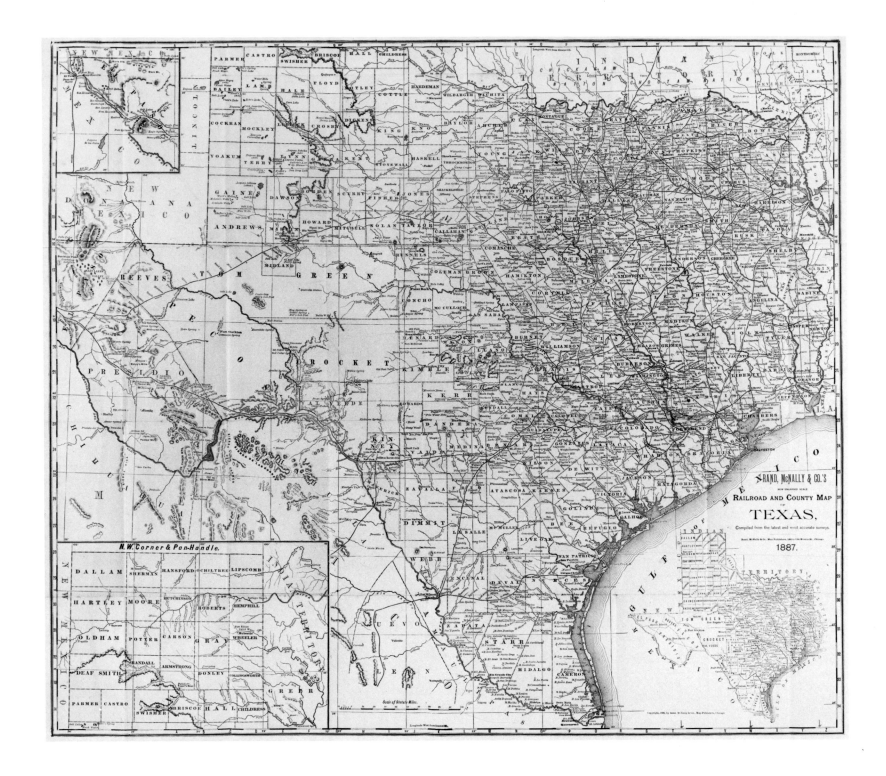

Plate 49.   Rand, McNally & Co., *Rand, McNally & Co.'s New Enlarged Scale Railroad and County Map of Texas* . . . (Chicago, 1887).

Cerograph; 65 × 73 cm (25.6 × 28.7 in.).

The City of Chicago allied itself quite early in its development with the emerging railroad industry, and the city soon became one of the largest railroad centers in the Midwest. In the 1850s, Chicago developed rapidly from a boom town to a metropolis, and one of the numerous Americans who streamed west to take advantage of the opportunities during that decade was a young printer from Boston, William H. Rand. Within ten years, Rand befriended another young printer, Irish immigrant Andrew McNally, and in 1868 the firm of Rand, McNally & Company was formed. It initially offered printing services of every kind, but soon came to specialize in the ready market of the railroad industry. They printed railroad schedules and tickets, and advertised a large variety of associated paraphernalia like conductor's punches and watches. In 1871 they began to produce a monthly publication detailing the developments in railroad companies, construction, business dealings, and schedules, called the *Western Railroad Guide*. By January 1873, they announced "a new era in the history of the *Guide*—that of the inauguration of map illustrations."

The era of railroad transportation and western migration created a great demand for Rand, McNally's maps and guidebooks; these same forces, however, rendered the product obsolete virtually overnight. The numbers of copies required also strained the limits of the traditional methods for producing such items. In short, there was a great demand for large numbers of accurate, inexpensive, up-to-date maps and guidebooks. To fill this demand it was necessary for Rand, McNally to adopt a new printing technology, cerography or wax-engraving, which produced a hard, durable plate that could be used in the new steam powered presses, but which could also be readily corrected and amended. The adoption and perfection of the wax-engraving process as a production technique had enormous influence on the growth of Rand, McNally.

Andrew McNally, III, a chief executive officer for the firm, once proclaimed that "the introduction of this single technique was responsible for the Company's success in map making." It has also had great influence on the development of the American map trade, not only because of the characteristic appearance of cerographic maps, but also because of the industrialization of the map making process it required. The result has been termed "the All-American Map."

Rand, McNally's guidebooks developed into a number of other products designed to serve the same market, including a series of *County and Railroad Pocket Maps and Shippers' Guides* for the several states. These works focused on the railroad lines linking towns and settlements in the developing West and became an important mainstay in the commerce of the region. They were constantly revised and updated, and frequently the new towns born from way stations, wood and water stops, and points of connection along the developing rail lines were formally recognized for the first time in these maps. The extension of the lines themselves, and the construction of spurs to serve developing industry, appeared on these maps as well. The maps were accompanied by a *Shippers' Guide*, which included an index to the maps in which the towns were located, as well as listings of train schedules and connections and the prevailing freight rates. When examined in a series, these Rand, McNally maps reveal the westward march of settlement as the railroads were extended, the counties organized, and the towns founded. They served as an aid to this process as it occurred and later served as an eloquent witness to it.

Cartographic History Library, The University of Texas at Arlington.

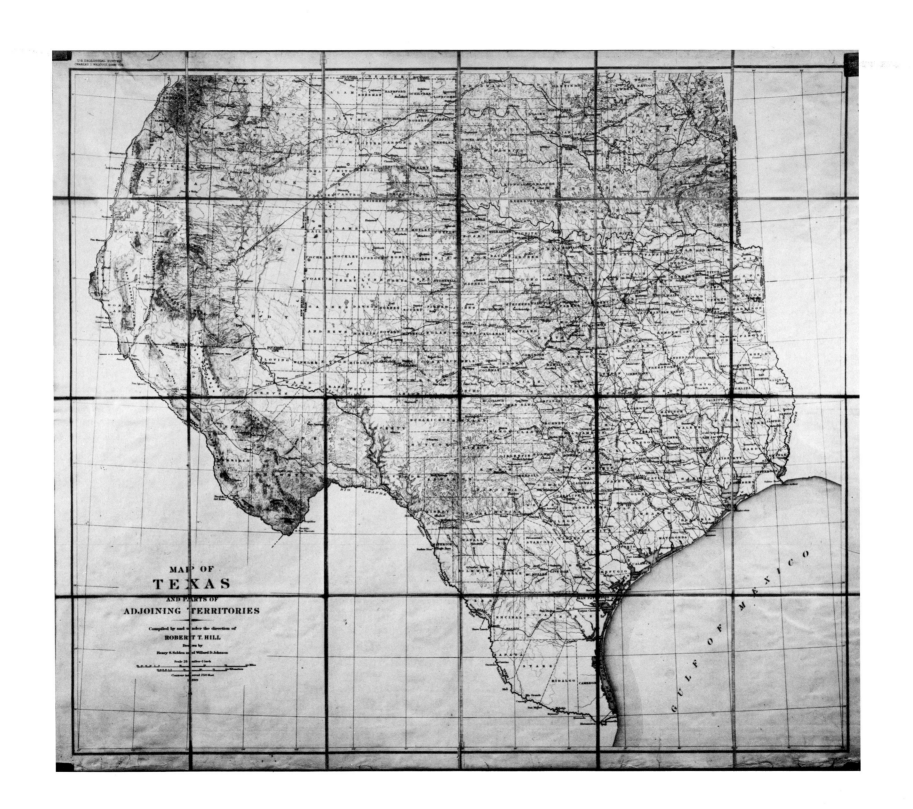

MAP OF
TEXAS
AND PARTS OF
ADJOINING TERRITORIES

Compiled by and under the direction of
ROBERT T. HILL

Drawn by
Henry S. Selden and Willard D. Johnson

Scale 25 miles=1 inch

Contour interval 250 feet

Plate 50. Robert T. Hill, *Map of Texas and Parts of the Adjoining Territories.*

Lithograph; 87 × 80 cm (34.2 × 31.5 in.). Published in: *Topographic Atlas of the United States. Physical Geography of the Texas Region* (Washington, 1900).

As the nineteenth century drew to a close, so too did the last stretches of unknown and unclaimed lands in the American West. While cartographers in the first part of the century had attemped to present the lands in outline form with scant interior information, cartographers at the end of the century were dealing with specific details of land surveys. Map makers were at last learning the physical characteristics of the land from actual experiences, and this information spurred new scientific interest in the topography and geology of these lands, which bore little resemblance to the eastern half of the nation.

The life and career of Robert T. Hill, a distinguished scholar, teacher, geologist, and Texas, spanned this remarkable transition period in knowledge of the geography of the nation and in the techniques of map making. Active in many of the geological surveys of the Rio Grande and Big Bend region, he often studied with John Wesley Powell, who had founded the United States Geological Survey. In his countless studies and publications, Hill presented previously unknown details of the greater Texas region. In 1899 Hill supervised the compilation and drawing of the *Map of Texas and Parts of Adjoining Territories . . .* , which he included in the *Topographic Atlas of the United States, Physical Geography of the Texas Region,* published by the United States Geological Survey in 1900. The map added new sophistication to Texas's cartographic history and helped to set new scientific standards in the mapping of the region.

As the diverse natural regions of Texas became well known, new challenges emerged for the cartographer. The mushrooming collections of cultural features and the invention of new transportation facilities had to be handled by the twentieth century map makers. But by the time of Hill's 1899 map, the lands of Texas had been discovered, charted, explored, mapped, and finally settled, bringing to an end one of the most unusual and significant chapters in the history of American cartography.

References: Day 1006, 1753.

SOURCES CITED

Baltimore Museum of Art. *The World Encompassed: an Exhibition of the History of Maps held at the Baltimore Museum of Art October 7 to November 23, 1952. . . .* Baltimore: Trustees of the Walters Art Gallery, 1951.
Cited as: *World Encompassed.*

James Perry Bryan and Walter Hanak. *Texas in Maps.* Austin: The University of Texas at Austin, 1961.
Cited as: Bryan and Hanak.

Carlos Eduardo Castañeda and Early Martin. *Three Manuscript Maps of Texas by Stephen F. Austin.* Austin: privately printed, 1930.
Cited as: Castañeda, *Three Manuscript Maps.*

James M. Day and Ann B. Dunlap. *The Map Collection of the Texas State Archives, 1527–1900.* Austin: Texas State Library, 1962.
Cited as: Day.

Henry Harrisse. *The Discovery of North America.* London: Henry Stevens and Son; and Paris: H. Walter. 1892.
Cited as: Harrisse, *CAV.*

Egon Klemp. *America in Maps, Dating from 1500 to 1856.* Leipzig: Edition Leipzig, 1976.
Cited as: Klemp.

Cornelius Koeman. *Atlantes Neerlandici: Bibliography of Terrestrial, Maritime, and Celestial Atlases and Pilot Books, Published in the Netherlands up to 1880.* Amsterdam: Theatrum Orbis Terrarum, 1967–69.
Cited as: Koeman.

———. *The Sea on Paper: The Story of the Van Keulens and their "Sea Torch."* Amsterdam: Theatrum Orbis Terrarum, 1972.
Cited as: Koeman, *Sea on Paper.*

Woodbury Lowery. *The Lowery Collection: A Descriptive List of Maps of the Spanish Possessions within the Present Limits of the United States, 1502–1820.* Washington: Government Printing Office, 1912.
Cited as: Lowery.

Malcolm Dallas McLean. *Papers Concerning Robertson's Colony in Texas.* Volume II. Fort Worth: Texas Christian University Press, 1975.
Cited as: McLean, *Papers.*

Lawrence Martin. "John Disturnell's Map of the United Mexican States." In Walter W. Ristow, *A la Carte: Selected Papers on Maps and Atlases.*

Washington: Library of Congress, 1972. Reprinted with extensive revisions from David Hunter. *Treaties and other International Acts of the United States of America.* Washington: Department of State, 1937.
Cited as: Martin, *Disturnell.*

Nils Adolf Erik Nordenskiold. *Facsimile-Atlas to the Early History of Cartography.* Stockholm: P. A. Norstedt, 1889.
Cited as: Nordenskiold.

Philip Lee Phillips. *A List of Geographical Atlases in the Library of Congress.* Washington: Government Printing Office, 1909–14.
Cited as: Phillips, *Atlases.*

———. *A List of Maps of America in the Library of Congress. . . .* Washington: Government Printing Office, 1901.
Cited as: Phillips, *Maps.*

Walter W. Ristow. "John Melish and His Map of the United States." Walter W. Ristow. *A la Carte: Selected Papers on Maps and Atlases.* Washington: Library of Congress, 1972. Reprinted from *Library of Congress Quarterly Journal of Current Acquisitions,* September 1962.
Cited as: Ristow, *Melish.*

Thomas Winthrop Streeter. *The Celebrated Collection of Americana Formed by the Late Thomas Winthrop Streeter. . . .* New York: Parke-Bernet Galleries, 1966.
Cited as: Streeter, *Sale.*

———. *Bibliography of Texas, 1795–1845.* Cambridge: Harvard University Press, 1955–60.
Cited as: Streeter, *Texas.*

Jacobo María del Pilár Carlos Manuel Stuart Fitz-James, 10th Duke of Berwick, *Mapas Españoles de America, siglos XV–XVII.* Madrid: privately printed, 1951.
Cited as: *Mapas Españoles.*

Ronald Vere Tooley. *California as an Island. . . .* London: Map Collectors' Circle, 1964.
Cited as: Tooley, *California.*

———. *French Mapping of America: the De l'Isle, Bauche, De Zauche Succession (1700–1830).* London: Map Collectors' Circle, 1967.
Cited as: Tooley, *Delisle.*

Henry Raup Wagner. *The Cartography of the Northwest Coast of America to the Year 1800.* Berkeley: University of California Press, 1937.
Cited as: Wagner, *Northwest Coast.*

Henry Raup Wagner and Charles L. Camp. *The Plains and the Rockies.* Columbus, Ohio: Long's College Book Company, 1953.
Cited as: *Wagner-Camp.*

Henry Raup Wagner. *The Spanish Southwest, 1542–1794.* Albuquerque: The Quivara Society, 1937.
Cited as: Wagner, *Spanish Southwest.*

Carl I. Wheat. *Mapping the Transmississippi West, 1540–1861.* San Fran-

cisco: Institute of Historical Cartography, 1957–63.
Cited as: Wheat.

Justin Winsor. *The Kohl Collection (now in the Library of Congress) of Maps Relating to America.* Washington: Government Printing Office, 1904.
Cited as: Kohl.

———. *Narrative and Critical History of America.* Boston: Houghton Mifflin and Company, 1884–89.
Cited as: Winsor.

SUGGESTIONS FOR FURTHER READING

It has been our hope from the beginning that our work on the maps in this book would stimulate increased interest, and perhaps research, in the cartographic history of Texas. The extent of the literature relating to the history of cartography is well represented by the size of the Library of Congress's *Bibliography of Cartography*, which now runs to five massive volumes plus a supplement. Unfortunately, little of this literature relates directly to the American Southwest, and most of what may be learned about that area must be gleaned from sources covering broader or peripheral topics. What follows is an extremely brief list that includes, for the most part, only those items readily available in any moderate-sized public library, or the libraries of most colleges and universities.

The best general introduction to the history of cartography remains Lloyd Brown's *The Story of Maps* (New York: Little, Brown, 1949). Brown, for many years the curator of the great map collection at the Clements Library at the University of Michigan, covers the entire subject in an erudite, but extremely readable fashion. The book includes a helpful bibliography and has been reprinted several times, most recently in paperback by Dover Publications (New York, 1979). Leo Bagrow's *History of Cartography*, originally published in German (Berlin: Springer-Verlag, 1951), is a much more comprehensive approach to the subject. It has been revised and extended by R. A. Skelton, long Keeper of Maps at the British Museum, and this English translation (London: C. A. Watts, 1964), remains the most authoritative general treatise. Skelton has also produced a number of valuable works in his own right, including *Maps: A Historical Survey of their Study and Collecting* (Chicago: The University of Chicago Press, 1972), *Decorative Printed Maps of the 15th to 18th Centuries* (London: Staples Press, 1952), and *Explorers' Maps* (London: Hamlyn Publishing Group, 1958).

The discussion of map printing in this book is based in large part on the information contained in *Five Centuries of Map Printing* (Chicago, The University of Chicago Press, 1975). That book is a series of articles by several authors and were presented as the Third Series of the Kenneth Nebenzahl, Jr., Lectures in the History of Cartography at the Herman Dunlap Smith Center for the History of Cartography at the Newberry Library in Chicago in 1972. They were edited for pub-

lication by David Woodward, Director of the Smith Center, and contain numerous helpful illustrations.

The best general reference for the map trade is probably Ronald Vere Tooley's *Maps and Mapmakers* (London: Batsford, 1949). It can also serve as a supplement to the above-cited general works on the history of cartography. The fifth edition of this valuable work appeared in 1979.

Although many of the above works contain some reproductions of the maps which are discussed, perhaps none perform this valuable service as well as the classic in the field, *A Book of Old Maps* (Cambridge: Harvard University Press, 1926), by Emerson David Fite and Archibald Freeman. Only about a quarter of the nearly one hundred maps reproduced in the volume pertain to Texas or the Southwest, but the work is extremely valuable nonetheless. It has been reprinted by Arno Press in 1969 and again in paperback by Dover Publications in 1974. Perusers of map dealers' catalogs will quickly become familiar with the reference "Fite and Freeman."

The history of the voyages of discovery and the initial exploration of the North American interior is available in authoritative and readable form from two sources. The late Admiral Samuel Eliot Morison's prize-winning *The Great Explorers* (New York: Oxford University Press, 1978) is an abridgement of his two-volume *European Discovery of America* (New York: Oxford University Press, 1971, 1974). David Beers Quinn provides an equally good summary and analysis in *North America from Earliest Discovery to the First Settlements* (New York: Harper and Row, 1977). Quinn has also edited a valuable compendium of original documents relating to early European activity in America, *New American World* (New York: Arno Press, 1979). Many of the important documents given in translation in this five volume set appeared earlier in Quinn's *North American Discovery* (New York: Harper and Row, 1971). These collections of documents serve to add the flavor of the contemporary civilizations to the narratives of the discoveries. An additional supplement to these historical narratives is provided by two additional works, *The Discovery of North America* (London: Elek, 1971), and *The Exploration of North America* (New York: Putnam, 1974); produced by Quinn, William P. Cumming, R. A. Skelton, and others, these two volumes are full of contemporary engravings and illustrations, as well as map reproductions, which graphically reveal the history related.

The list of Sources Cited which precedes the reproductions in this book includes several valuable annotated lists which, in addition to giving full citations and descriptions to the maps themselves, often provide important additional information. Lowery and Kohl both contain extensive notations, by Philip Lee Phillips and Justin Winsor respectively, that often give clues to further information. Unfortunately, both of these sources have been long out of print. Koeman's *Atlantes Neerlandici,* in addition to having the most exhaustive possible descriptions of the atlases, gives important biographies and trade histories of the dominant Dutch chart and map makers. The list of Sources Cited also includes the only three definitive works of regional scope concerning the cartographic history of North America: Wagner in the Northwest, Cumming in the Southeast, and Wheat in the Trans-Mississippi West. All three of these works are extremely important contributions, but none deals directly with Texas or the Southwest. Wheat comes nearest in scope, but he specifically excludes consideration of localities in favor of an overview of the entire West, and consequently rarely mentions Texas. Only Streeter's *Bibliography of Texas* deals directly with the contents of this volume and, though his listings are extremely informative and helpful, the brief fifty year span of the work covers scarcely more than ten percent of the scope of this book.

In fact, aside from Streeter, there are only four separately published works which deal directly with Texas maps. James Day's listing of the collection in the State Archives is interesting, but contains no annotations. Castañeda's *Three Manuscript Maps* is restricted to a brief analysis of some of Stephen F. Austin's manuscript maps, and is not readily available having been privately printed in an edition of only fifty copies. *Contours of Discovery,* which the authors of this volume produced for the Texas State Historical Association, is aimed primarily at the student of Texas history. It contains a folio of color reproductions of twenty important historical maps of Texas together with an accompanying guide. J. P. Bryan and Walter Hanak's brief catalog to an exhibition of maps mounted in the Humanities Research Center at The University of Texas at Austin in 1961 was the first to treat the subject of the mapping of Texas as worthy of interest and inquiry. And in that work is perhaps the genesis of the present, for the authors must acknowledge that their own interest in Texas maps was begun through their association with James Perry Bryan. If our volume has a similar influence on another researcher, we will be pleased.

INDEX

MAPS OF TEXAS AND THE SOUTHWEST
was designed by Emmy Ezzell.
Type was composed at the
University of New Mexico Printing Plant
in Goudy Old Style
with Goudy Handtooled display
from G & S Typesetters.
It was printed on 100-lb. Westvaco Celesta Litho Gloss,
and bound in Whitman Imperial Bonded Leather
and Holliston Sail Cloth,
at Kingsport Press.